Grace Llewellyn is a former middle school English teacher. Her experience of teaching in public and private schools in the USA and her encounter with the work of educator John Holt led her to the conclusion that teenagers needed their own book about homeschooling. *The Teenage Liberation Handbook* is her first book.

THE TEENAGE LIBERATION HANDBOOK

How to Quit School and get a Real Life and Education

GRACE LLEWELLYN

ELEMENT
Shaftesbury, Dorset,
Rockport, Massachusetts
Melbourne, Victoria

© Element Books Limited 1997
Text © Grace Llewellyn 1997

First published in Great Britain in 1997 by
Element Books Limited
Shaftesbury, Dorset SP7 8BP

Published in the USA in 1997 by
Element Books, Inc.
PO Box 830, Rockport, MA 01966

Published in Australia in 1997 by
Element Books and distributed
by Penguin Books Australia Ltd
487 Maroondah Highway, Ringwood,
Victoria 3134

Cover design by Max Fairbrother
Page design by Roger Lightfoot
Typeset by Bournemouth Colour Press
Printed and bound in Great Britain
by J W Arrowsmith Ltd, Bristol

British Library Cataloguing in Publication
data available

Library of Congress Cataloging in Publication
Llewellyn Grace.
The teenage liberation handbook: how to quit school and get a
real life and education/Grace Llewellyn. — [Rev. ed.]
p. cm.
Includes bibliographical references and index.
ISBN 1–86204–104–0 (pbk.: alk. paper)
1. Self-culture. 2. Home schooling—United States. 3. Dropouts—
United States. 4. Non-formal education—United States. I. Title.
LC32.L54 1997
371.04'2—dc21 97–19785
CIP

ISBN 1–86204–104–0

This is a revised edition of a book of the same title published by Lowry
House, Eugene, Oregon in 1991.

Contents

Part 3: The Tailor-made Educational Extravaganza

Part 4: Touching the World – Finding Good Work

Thanks

In writing this book, I stood on the shoulders of a giant. John Holt's visionary, compassionate books on education and unschooling opened my eyes and clarified my beliefs. He died in 1985, two years before I even heard of him. Nevertheless, like most people whose lives are changed by his books, I think of him as a personal friend. Without his work this book wouldn't have been possible. I wouldn't have thought of it, let alone written it. Many of my ideas throughout this book are built directly on his.

I am also extremely grateful to the homeschooling community – the thousands of people who have taken John's ideas and turned them into reality. Without their examples, my book would be flat, hypothetical, and utopian. They give the rest of us a beginning sense of what's possible without schools.

More than a hundred teenagers filled out my lengthy questionnaire on unschooling, some in great detail, and the parents who have written me insightful letters and invited me to their homes are too numerous to list. For this revised edition, more teenagers and parents kindly wrote about their experiences.

The generous visionaries at Holt Associates gave me permission to use material from *Growing Without Schooling* magazine, and this material helps me to show, again and again, the range of activities possible for a person unrestricted by school.

Huge thanks to the many hundreds of people who wrote me letters after reading the first edition of this book – sharing the stories of their lives, encouraging and inspiring me, sending money and handpainted cards and gifts, and continuing to teach me about unschooling.

I am grateful to the parents, teenagers and others all over Planet Earth who wrote to me about international homeschooling: Kyoko Aizawa, Janine Banks, Debbie Bennett, Jan Brownlie, Sarah Cashmore, Lantien Chu, Konomi Shinohara Corbin, Kate Durham, Elizabeth Edwards, Sophie Haesen, Carolyn Hamilton, Katherine Hebert, Marie Heitzmann, Debra Kempt, Karen Maxwell, Roland Meighan, Valerie Bonham Moon, Pat Montgomery, Bippan Norberg, Maureen Normoyle, Robert Ozmak, Lyndon Pugh, Monica Reid, Candis Ritsey, Aleta Shepler, Sally Sherman, Brenda J Smith, Eleanor Sparks, Denise Sutherland, Lomi Szil, Candace Thayer-Coe, Margy Walter, Kim Wark and Jill Whitmore.

Thanks to the college admissions officers and professors who shared their opinions and advice, and the people from various organizations who patiently answered my questions and sent information.

I am grateful to friends and family for support both personal and intellectual: Gary Oakley, Heiko Koester, Clement Cheung, Kris Shapiro, Dick Ruth, Josanna Crawford, Richard Llewellyn, Heather Llewellyn, Heather Diefenderfer, Colleen Llewellyn, Kelly Rains, Mark Llewellyn, Othman Llewellyn and Caroline Diston.

My assistant Janet Taylor provided energetic help in preparing this revised edition, and brightened many days.

Susannah Sheffer, editor of *Growing Without Schooling*, has been a constant source of inspiration and enlightenment. I thank her for her vision, her clear and persevering intellect, and her unwavering friendship.

My brother Ned Llewellyn made many 45-mile trips to my house during moments of computer crisis; I don't know how I'd manage without him.

Thanks to Jennifer Day, my editor at Element Books, for believing in my work and helping to spread the word to teenagers all over this planet.

From my heart, I thank my parents, whose love, trust, and support has buttressed so much of my life. And most especially I thank my true love Skip: autodidact, dinner cook, best friend and soulmate.

Introduction

First, A Nice Little Story

On a soft green planet, a smiling baby was born in an orchard resplendent with every kind of fruit in the universe. The baby's parents called her Tanika, and Tanika spent her days roaming the warm wet ground on hands and knees. Spotting a clump of gulberries off in the distance, she'd crawl after it and crush the sweet fruit in her mouth, red juice staining her brown chin and neck. A muavo would fall fatly from the high crown of the muavo tree, and she'd savor its golden tang. Each day revealed new wonders – bushapples, creamy labanas, the nutty crunch of the brown shrombart. The orchard's fruit sparkled in the dew and sun like thousands of living moist jewels against the green fragrance of cushioning leaves.

As her eyes grew stronger Tanika lifted her gaze. The opulent branches above her hung heavy with fruits she'd never dreamed of, globular and glistening. Tanika's mother and father sometimes wandered the orchard too, and she watched them reach out easily and take a shining cluster here, a single green satinplum there. She'd watch them eat and imagine being tall enough to roam and reach as freely as they.

Sometimes one of them would bend down and give Tanika one of those fruits from up there in the moving leaves. Fresh from the branches, it intoxicated her, and her desire to know and taste all the fruits of the orchard so consumed her that she began to long for the day she could reach that far.

Her longing strengthened her appetite, and the fruit strengthened her legs, and one day Tanika crawled to the base of a mysterious bush at the edge of the stream that watered the orchard. She leaned carefully forward and braced her arms as she positioned her feet. Unsteadily she rose and groped for the shrub's pale fruit. Tugging knocked her off balance and she sat down hard in an overripe muavo, but she barely noticed the fruit squishing under her thighs: in her hands she grasped a fruit thin-skinned and silver, fresh and new. She pressed it to her nose and face before she let her teeth puncture it.

No sooner had she tossed the smooth kernel into the stream than she heard a rustling behind her. A jolly bespectacled face grinned down at her.

'Well, well, well! You're a mighty lucky little girl! I've come to teach you to get the fruit down from the tall trees!'

Tanika's happiness unfurled like a sail. She could hardly believe her good luck. Not only had she just picked and eaten her first bush fruit, but here was a man she didn't even know offering to show her how to reach the rainbow of treats high above her head. Tanika was so overcome with joy that she immediately rose to her feet again, and plucked another of the small moonish fruits.

The jolly stranger slapped the fruit from Tanika's wrist. Stunned, she fell again and watched her prize roll into the stream. 'Oh dear,' said the man, 'You've already picked up some bad habits. That may make things difficult.' The slapping hand now took Tanika's and pulled her up. Holding on this way, Tanika stumbled along behind the stranger.

She wanted to ask questions, like, 'Why didn't you just show me how to pick those berries hanging above the bush where I was?' But she kept her mouth shut. If she was going off to pick the high fruit, she supposed it didn't matter where, or that she'd sacrificed her one beautiful moonfruit. Maybe they were going to a special tree melting with juicing fruits, branches bent almost to the ground, low enough for her outstretched fingers. Yes! That must be it. Excitement renewed, she moved her legs faster. The stranger grinned and squeezed her hand.

Soon Tanika saw the biggest, greyest thing she'd ever laid eyes on. In quiet fascination she tripped along as they stepped off the spongy humus of the orchard floor on to a smooth pavement. 'Here we are!' beamed the guide. They entered the building, full of odd smells and noises. They passed through a pair of heavy black doors, and the man pushed Tanika into a loud, complicated room full of talking children and several adults. She looked at the children, some sitting on the floor, some crawling about or walking. All of them had trays or plates in front of them heaped with odd mushy lumps of various colors. Also, some of the children were busy coloring simple pictures of fruits, and some wore badges and tags on their shirts in the shape of fruit. Baffled, Tanika tried to work out what the children were doing in such a dark, fruitless place, what the lumpy stuff was, and above all, why her guide had stopped here on their way to the bountiful tree.

But before she had time to think, two things happened. First, one of the kids took something metal and used it to scoop a lump of dull pinkish stuff into his mouth. Tanika opened her mouth in panic to warn the kid. Maybe there was something wrong with him; he was much bigger than she was, old enough to know better. But just as she began to yell, a new hand, smooth, pulled her up again. 'OK, Tanika,' said the cheery woman that went with the hand, 'This is the cafeteria. We're looking forward to helping you grow, and we're certain we can help you to pick tree fruit, as long as you do your part.'

Tanika felt confused. She didn't see what this place could have to do with picking gulberries, and at that moment she was particularly hungry for more of that shining moonfruit. But she had no time to think. The smooth-handed woman put Tanika on a cold chair at a table. 'Here,' she said, and nudged a box of crayons and a black outline of a plum at her. 'Today you will color this, and it will help you get ready for eating tomorrow.' Tanika started to feel foolish.

She'd never guessed that learning to pick fruit would be so complicated. She colored the plum with all the colors in the box, trying in vain to make it round and enticing like the fruits of the orchard.

The rest of the day passed in a daze. Tanika was made to color more of the pictures, and to her disgust most of the children ate the formless mush on the plates in front of them. Some of the fat and greasy children asked for more and stuffed themselves. Whenever this happened, the adults ran in and put gold stars all over the kid's arms and face. Many things happened – children fought, napped, sat quietly fidgeting with the stuff. Finally, the jolly man took Tanika's hand and led her out of the dark building. As her bare feet met the orchard grass, she caught the scent of ripe labana. She asked the stranger if he would get one for her, but he merely laughed.

Tanika was far too confused to put any of her questions into words. By the time they arrived at the tree where Tanika slept with her parents, the evening light had turned the leaves to bronze, and she was exhausted. Too tired to look for fruit, she fell asleep and dreamed fitfully.

In the morning her mind was clear. She still wanted to reach the high fruit, but she did not want to go back to the noisy smelly dark cafeteria. She could already reach the bushfruit; maybe in time she'd grasp the high fruit too.

But when the bespectacled person arrived, he told her that she'd never reach the trees without many years in the cafeteria. He explained it: 'You can't reach them now, can you?' and 'Your parents can reach them. That's because they went to the cafeteria. I can reach them, because I went to the cafeteria.' Tanika had no time to think this through, because he'd pulled her to her feet again and they were off. She hadn't had time to find breakfast, and her stomach rumbled painfully.

Tanika went in the room and sat down politely. 'Please,' she asked one of the adults, 'can you help me pick tree fruits today? That's why I'm here, and also today I didn't have time for breakfast.'

The tall lady laughed. 'Well, well, well! Aren't we cute! *Tree* fruit! Before you're ready for tree fruit, you have to prepare!' She disappeared behind a curtain and returned carrying a tray with a scoop of greenish stuff. Tanika jerked back. She looked round wildly for an escape route. Out of the corner of her eye she saw a boy watching with soft dark quiet eyes. The lady grabbed her hand.

'Don't be afraid, Tanika,' she laughed. 'How will you ever work up to eating tree fruit if you can't handle plate fruit?' She put the tray on the table, and took the metal thing, spooning up a piece of the stuff and holding it in front of the small girl. Tanika pushed the spoon away violently. Then she put her head down on the table and cried.

The lady's voice changed. 'So you're going to be a tough one, Tanika? Just remember, you're only hurting yourself when you refuse to eat. If you want to succeed, you'd better do as we ask.' She walked away.

When Tanika stopped crying, her stomach was desperately empty. She sat up and looked at the tray. She was afraid of the stuff. She bent down to smell it and caught a faint, stale whiff of limbergreen berry. The smell, even distorted, was a familiar friend. She picked up the spoon and ate her first bite of cafeteria food.

Tanika was relieved. Although the goop was slimy, far too sweet, and mostly tasteless, it wasn't nearly as bad as it looked. And it did seem to be made from limbergreen berries. She ate it all, and felt a little better. The lady came back. 'Very good,' she smiled. She stuck a green star on the back of Tanika's hand. 'We'll do some more exercises and then later on you can try something new to eat.'

Hours later, Tanika had been the apple in 'Velcro the Stem on the Apple', and had drawn a muavo tree and listened to an older student explain what fruits contained vitamins P,

Q and Z. Apparently she had done all these things right, because the lady came back and put more green and gold stars on her hands and cheeks. Some of the children looked at her angrily, though, so perhaps she'd done something wrong.

At this point a man rang a little bell. Immediately all the children sat down at the tables and folded their hands neatly. A girl grabbed Tanika's hand and shoved her on to a chair. Then six children walked into the room carrying stacks of trays. They put one in front of each child, and Tanika saw that each tray contained five purple and blue wafers. 'Yum!' said the girl next to Tanika, 'Violetberry cakes!' Tanika jumped. She'd seen her parents eat violetberries, and also seen the accompanying ecstasy on their faces. She easily pictured the graceful coniferous trees on which they grew.

She picked up a wafer. It was warm, but not with the gentle warmth of the sun. She put it in her mouth. Dry, sandy ... she chewed obediently but sadly. This was it? Disappointment sank her stomach and she put the cake down, mentally crossing violetberries off her wishlist forever.

In the end Tanika was made to eat the violetberry cake – all five hunks of it – before the bespectacled man would lead her out of the door. Her stomach throbbed all the way home. That night she crawled into her mother's arms and sobbed. Her mother rocked her, then whispered something to Tanika's father. He disappeared, and returned a minute later with an armload of tiny, glowing violetberries.

'It's time,' said her mother sweetly, 'For your first fresh violetberries.'

Her father dangled them teasingly above her lips, but Tanika only cried harder. The berries' fragrance, though delicate and sweet, clashed with her distended heavy stomach. She was far too full, and it was violetberries' fault. Both parents teased and offered, but they finally gave up.

The mother laid Tanika down to rest alone, and the two adults stood whispering while the moon rose, worry in their voices.

At the cafeteria the next day the adults met Tanika with an unpleasant stare. 'You're making things difficult for yourself,' scolded the woman with smooth hands. 'Your parents have reported that your attitude at home is not meeting standards for girls your age. You need to eat *much* more thoroughly.' A girl brought a plate crowded with dried out, wrinkly little fruits. Tanika ate them, tough and tasteless. Her stomach hurt again. After they dissected a preserved bushapple, she ate another trayful of canned gulberry. Then she went back home and slept.

Days passed, and months. Tanika ate obediently and earned lots of stars. There was a picture of a bright green tree painted on one of the walls, and when the whole roomful of children ate their food quickly, the adults had them play a game. They stuck three or four cut-out paper fruits to the tree, and then the kids were made to take turns jumping or reaching to try to take them. Whoever reached a fruit got to keep it, and also was called a winner and plastered with dozens of gold stars.

One day when the bespectacled man walked her home he told her the cafeteria would be closed for two days for cleaning. He handed her a little white carton and said, 'Be sure to eat all of this while I'm gone, and I'll pick you up in two days.'

As he waddled away, a strange inspiration seized Tanika's brain. She touched her swollen belly and flung the carton away. Out of it tumbled cakes, red mush and hard little biscuits smelling flatly of labanas.

When she woke the next morning her stomach rumbled and she got up to look for breakfast. Leaving the clearing, she accidentally kicked a biscuit. Out of habit, she picked it up and almost put it in her mouth, then caught herself and aimed instead for a bush full of gulberries. Furtively she snatched a handful and crushed them to her lips. Sweet and wild, they made her want to sing.

Tanika's father saw her then, and called excitedly to her mother. Both of them ran to their child and squeezed her. 'Look what you've learned at the cafeteria!' cried her mother. 'My baby is growing up!'

'Be sure to eat all your homefood,' said her father, 'So you won't be behind when you go back.' Then his tone of voice changed. 'What's that?' he said. He sprinted off and grabbed up the white carton. Tanika watched in horror as he searched the orchard floor. A few minutes later he returned with everything – biscuits, cake, mush.

Tanika ate it all.

The cafeteria opened again and Tanika went back. Every day she ate faster, and gradually stopped resisting, even in her own mind. One day she reached the highest paper fruit on the painted tree. All the adults patted her head and she could barely see her brown skin under all the gold stars. She started walking to the cafeteria every day by herself. The adults started giving her food for the evenings, and usually she'd eat it like they said. One day, walking home, she flung her hands to the sky and they touched, accidentally, a muavo hanging down from its branch. Tanika jumped back. 'I can pick it,' she said slowly. 'It worked.' She thought for a minute. The cooks had said it would happen, some day, if she ate what they gave her and jumped as high as she could during the tree game.

Tanika gracefully severed the muavo from its stem, examined it, and tossed it neatly into a shadow.

She wasn't hungry.

The Note to Parents

Against the advice of lots of people, I didn't write this book for you. I wrote it for teenagers. I wrote it for teenagers because I wished that when I was a teenager someone had written it for me. I wrote it for teenagers because my memory and experience insist that they are as fully human as adults. I wrote it for teenagers because I found an appalling dearth of respectful, serious nonfiction for them. In short, I wrote it for teenagers because they are the experts on their own lives.

No, I have not forgotten your child's 'place.' I know that if you want to, you can probably prevent him or her leaving school. I have written this book anyway, in the hope that after careful thought, you will see fit to honor the choice he or she makes.

Yes, if your son or daughter leaves school, it will change your life. If the experiences of pioneering homeschoolers can predict your future, you will see family relationships deepen; teenagers without eight hours of school and homework have time to make friends with their parents. You will see family relationships heal, uncomplicated by displaced anger about school. You will feel less harshly evaluated according to teenage fashion magazine standards. Depending on your own background and schooling, you may undergo a period of depression, anger and bitterness. *You* went to school, after all, and in contrast to your children's unexpected freedom you may feel overwhelmed by a sense of loss – all the things you could have done with that time, all the choices you never thought you had, all the labels that stuck when schoolpeople put them on you. This funk, if you get it, will eventually give way to a new sense of freedom – at least mine did. You can't change the past, but you can change the present. You can peel the labels off, you can start making real choices, you have the rest of your life to *live*.

Homeschooling parents of teenagers are rarely 'teachers', in the school sense of the word, and this book never suggests that you forsake your own career or interests in order to learn a subject (like calculus) fast enough to 'teach' it. Healthy kids can teach themselves what they need to know, through books, other people, thinking and so on. (A freshly unschooled person may at *first* be a rotten learner; like cigarettes, school-style passivity can be a slow habit to kick.)

Nevertheless, you will probably find yourself more involved than before with your son's or daughter's education. If you have helped with or supervised your children's homework, or stayed in close touch with their teachers, homeschooling need not drain your energy any more than that. Your role will change, however. No longer is it your job to nag or lecture; instead, you answer questions and help find people or resources to answer the questions that you can't answer. Instead, when your daughter starts sketching castles, you introduce her to the architect you know or tell her about the lecture on medieval life that you saw advertised in the paper.

If an unschooled teenager doesn't need *teaching* from you, what does he or she need from you? *Parenthood*, of course, and all the love and stability therein.

Also, help with logistics, as implied in the castle example above. Few people can immediately take complete responsibility for their educations after being forcefully spoonfed for years. Please be willing to make some phone calls to set up meetings or lessons, to tell your kid about events or resources he might not otherwise know about, to draw a map to the planetarium or explain how to use the university library. Also, you will need to accompany your son or daughter through the homeschooling legal requirements of your state or country. Fortunately, there are support groups to help you make sense of this process.

Also, trust. When you tell your daughter about that forthcoming lecture on medieval life, make it clear that you are simply passing on information, not giving an assignment. If you don't believe in her, it won't work. If you give up on her, snoop, push or frequently anxiously inquire into the status of her algebraic knowledge, you will destroy any chance you had for a healthy family relationship, and you will send her right back to school, where there is so much less for her to lose.

Part of trusting means respecting your teenager's need for transition time. As chapter 11 of this book points out, new unschoolers often need time to work through a flood of feelings about school and life, before they can start attending to things 'intellectual' or 'academic'. Ride out the storm with your child. Offer your support, your ideas, your arms. Don't rush him.

Do I expect you to swallow all this? Not now; not by reading this short note. Later, yes. I expect you to change your mind in favour of unschooling by 1) reading books by John Holt, 2) reading *Growing Without Schooling* and other publications about unschooling, 3) reviewing your own adolescence and your present life and 4) humbly observing your teenaged child, allowing for the possibility that she might be a person ... like you.

Finally, on a different note: if you are already disillusioned by your child's 'education', or even sympathetic to the cause of unschooling, and if you live with a stuck or depressed teenager, I hope this book can be your ally in offering her or him some vision for healthy, self-directed change.

Best wishes.

About This Book

Did your class teacher or guidance counselor ever tell you to consider leaving school? That you have other choices, quite beyond lifelong hamburger flipping or inner-city crack dealing? That legally you can find a way out of school, that once you're out you'll learn and grow better, faster, and more naturally than you ever did in school, that there are zillions of alternatives, that you can quit school and still go to A Good College and even have a Real Life in the Suburbs if you so desire? Just in case no one ever told you these things, I'm going to. That's what this book is for.

WHAT IT'S NOT

This is not a book about the kind of 'homeschooling' in which you stay at home all day, hang a blackboard in the living room and write essays designed by your father or work geometry problems assigned by your mother. There are some good things to say about that kind of homeschooling, especially for young children who haven't yet acquired basic skills in reading, writing and arithmetic. There are also some bad things to say about it. In this book I will say little about it.

Most people who do fantastic unschoolish things with their time call themselves homeschoolers, because it keeps them out of trouble and it doesn't freak out the neighbors. Anne Brosnan put it well in a letter to *Growing Without Schooling* magazine (no. 73):

When an adult comes up and asks, 'Why aren't you in school?' you're supposed to soften it by saying, 'My mom (or dad) teaches me at home.' If you say, 'I don't even *go* to school. So far, I've taught myself everything I want to know,' they think you've run away from school or are a lunatic. Whereas the other way, they think your parent's a teacher and you get private lessons.

The usual adult person in America thinks it's terribly hard to teach yourself something, and if you want to learn something, you've got to find somebody to teach it to you. This leads to the idea that kids are dumb unless taught or unless they go to school.

If you give up school, you too will probably wish to call yourself a homeschooler, at least when you talk to the school board. But that doesn't require bringing the ugliness of school into your home, or transforming your parents into teachers. Nor, for that matter, does it require that you stay home. The idea is to catch more of the world, not less. To avoid these kinds of connotations, I usually use the term 'unschooling'. But be aware that many people who talk about 'homeschooling' mean the same thing I do when I say 'unschooling'.

This is not a book specifically about Christian homeschooling, although most Christians will find it as useful as anyone else. I point this out because many people associate homeschooling with fundamentalist Christianity and Fear of Darwin. Many homeschoolers *are* fundamentalist Christians which has a serious effect on what they do instead of *school* school. Many others, however, are agnostics, mellow Christians, Muslims, Hindus, Rastafarians, Jews, pagans, atheists and Buddhists. Help yourself to any religious belief you like, but in these pages I won't be suggesting that you read your Bible instead of a biology book.

WHAT IT IS

This book is a wild card, a shot in the dark, a hopeful prayer.

This book wants you to leave school and do what you love. Yes, I know, that's the weirdest thing you ever heard. Hoping to make this idea feel possible to you, I tell about teenagers who are already living happy lives without school, and I offer lots of ideas and strategies to help you get a real life and convince your adults to cooperate.

'Excuse me?' you interrupt. 'Leave school? Right! And throw away my future and pound the supermarket till all my life and get Addicted to Drugs and be totally lost in today's world? Right!'

If you said that, please feel free to march straight to the nearest schoolteacher and receive a bushel of gold stars, extra credit points and proud smiles. You've learned exactly what they taught you. After you get tired of sticking stars to your locker, do please come back and read further.

This book is built on the belief that life is wonderful and schools are stifling. It is built on an impassioned belief in freedom. And it is built on the belief that schools do the opposite of what they say they do. They prevent learning and they destroy one's love of learning.

Of course, there are hundreds of other books with a similar premise. Some of these books go on to suggest that if certain changes were made, or smarter teachers were hired, schools would be good places. Other books say compulsory schools are fundamentally bad places and society, or at least individual people, should abandon them. This book agrees with that, but it doesn't stop there.

This is a practical book – a book for individual teenagers, a real-life handbook meant to be used and acted on. I have no hope that the school system will change enough to make schools healthy places, until it makes school blatantly optional. But I have plenty of faith that people – you, your friends – can intelligently take greater control over their own lives. So this book bypasses the rigid, uncreative red tape of that system and instead speaks directly to you.

WHOM IT'S FOR

As the title gently implies, this is a book for teenagers, though their parents and little brothers are welcome too. If you are 9 and want to use this book to get free, more power to you. If you are 11 and think of yourself as a teenager, that's fine with me too.

Is this book for all teenagers? Here are four answers.

If you are like me, this book is definitely for you. When I was at school, people asked me if I liked it. Sometimes I said yes. Sometimes I said no. I didn't think about it much, because I thought it didn't matter. Whether I liked it or not, I knew (or thought I knew) there were no other options. I believed in school in an abstract sense – education, learning, great writers and poets and thinkers and all that. My grades were good. I hated homework – and rarely did any – but I felt constantly guilty, rather than proud, about this. I wasn't offended by the disrespect my peers and I lived with, because I'd never imagined that it was possible for adults to treat me differently.

Usually, I thought I'd be fine if only I was a senior instead of an eighth grader, or if only I went to some artsy boarding school instead of boring Capital High School. I liked about half my teachers, but felt no enthusiasm for their classes. I craved Friday afternoons and June. Except for choir, my life in school was dreary and uninspired, but I had nothing to compare it to. I'd never heard of homeschooling, let alone unschooling, and dropping out was not on my List of Possibilities in Life. I wonder now, sometimes with bitterness, how things might have been if I had heard then of the possibilities beyond school. The first wave of the unschooling movement caught some people about my age, and I envy them.

Very definitely, this book is *not* just for people who are labelled gifted. I make this point because in these pages you will run into a lot of examples of unschooled teenagers who do rather impressive things with their time. I don't want you to be intimidated by them, only inspired. They don't live brilliantly because they are smarter than you; they live brilliantly because they have the time and encouragement they need. Many of them did very badly at school before their parents set them free.

If you have already considered leaving school – as a 'dropout' or anything else – of course this book is for you. If you have been feeling guilty or inadequate because of your 'failure' in school, perhaps I can knock some optimistic sense into you. Perhaps I can get you to think of yourself as 'rising out' instead of dropping out. (I got this terminology from Herb Hough's letter in *Growing Without Schooling* magazine no. 79.) The way we think of ourselves makes all the difference.

This book is for you whether you live in the USA, Wales, Peru, South Africa, or anywhere else on Planet Earth. I wrote the first edition with only the US in mind, and many of these pages reflect my experience as a US citizen. But, as chapter 10 points out, unschooling is a growing trend in many far corners of the globe, and you can be part of it.

If you truly enjoy school and all its paraphernalia more than anything else you can possibly imagine doing, I suppose I'm not writing for you, because I don't under-stand you. I'm not sure you exist, but if you do, we live in different universes. I used to think everyone was strong willed and independently inclined. Now I'm not sure. Sometimes I think perhaps school really does completely destroy that fierce, free spirit in some people. Other times my mother half convinces me that some people are naturally docile and passive. Maybe I have something to learn about docility. Or maybe I have a healthy aversion to something dead in people that should be alive.

However, I invite you to have a look at this book anyway. Even if it doesn't change the way you think about school, it might make you aware of some useful opportunities and resources – things you can do with your life in addition to school. After you finish your homework, naturally.

Of course, some places we call school are less schoolish than others. I feel pretty strongly that even the most alternative school, as long as it is compulsory, is not a healthy place to be. But I'd be an idiot to say every single school is bad for every single person. If you go to a humane school, and love it, even in May, and have a gut feeling that it's a good and healthy place, stay there. I hope I never tell anyone to ignore their gut feelings. I always listen to mine, and usually act on them. Of course, you have to make sure you're not confusing fear and deeply imbedded guilt with your true feelings.

WHY I WROTE IT

Just in case you are dying to know.

When I went to college, I knew from the start that I wanted to be an English teacher. I had always loved to read and write, but I had rarely enjoyed any of the work I had done in my English classes. In my naivety, I blamed this on my teachers. Several of them were obviously very intelligent, interesting and creative people, but their classes were nevertheless dull, and I thought this was their fault. I knew I would be a different kind of teacher.

My own classes would be dynamic, entertaining and always engaging. I would love the stimulation of being around 'learning' all my life, and my students would shower me with continual gratitude for rescuing them from the brain-death of their previous existence.

Student teaching took some of the sparkle out of that arrogance, but I chalked up my victims' lack of complete enthusiasm to my inexperience and lack of adequate time to prepare. (Somehow, I assumed that later I'd have more time to prepare.) Yes, a few of them said I was the best teacher they'd ever had. Most of them just handed in most of their homework on time and looked at me in a funny way when I rhapsodized about writing. I did not find a real teaching position for the autumn after college graduation, and I ended up substitute teaching in the public (state) schools of Oakland and Berkeley, California.

Subbing put me in the position to see the ugliest aspects of school, and my lifelong tendency to rebel against or at least make fun of authority surfaced and grew. In between sending students to the office for calling me a 'white bitch' or for pinching me or for loudly interrupting too many times, I'd sit and despairingly ponder the meaninglessness of these huge inner-city schools. I still felt that, with determination, I could make a difference. However, I began to realize that working with the kinds of administrators I most often encountered could only be an uphill battle. Furthermore, for many of these students it was probably too late – schools had so crushed their love of learning that I could hardly hope to inspire all of them to write or think or discover wonderful things.

After that school year, I took a break to travel in Peru and then spent three months as a substitute teacher in the homogeneous, well-behaved schools that I grew up in in Boise, Idaho. I still felt that I wanted to teach kids to read and write but I began to yearn to escape the rigidity and dullness of public schools. I began contemplating starting my own tiny, inexpensive, independent school. I imagined a group of about ten students who spent their time taking field trips and hanging out in someone's basement making films or writing novels. While I was brainstorming and researching the logistics of setting up something like this, I first stumbled across the writing of John Holt. By that time I'd heard of homeschooling but dismissed it, as most people seem to, as the activity of a bunch of scaredy-cat fanatics afraid their kids would find out about evolution and condoms if they went to school. John Holt's writings threw a bright new light on the subject, and on the concepts of school and learning.

Essentially, he argued that learning is a natural process that happens to anyone who is busy doing something real for its own sake, and that school destroys and confuses this process. Although most of his ideas had never occurred to me, they immediately made so much sense that I felt as though I'd thought of them myself. His books were eloquent yet simple, by far the wisest words I had ever found about education. I realized that although a tiny school like the one I'd envisioned might be a good alternative for students, I wasn't equipped to start it – I didn't have any real expertise, and I didn't know anything worth teaching besides how to embroider, go backpacking, bake bread, dance a little, play the piano and maybe write. I realized how few skills I had, and that the few skills I *did* have hadn't come from school. I knew about a lot of things from reading and keeping my ears open, but few of the books that had shaped my mind had been assigned or recommended in school. I felt freshly angry about having given up ballet (instead of school) when I was 13, and about having pushed that biggest love of mine, dancing, into a mostly neglected cupboard. Mainly, I felt flooded by a sense of loss and bitterness – all that time I'd wasted sitting and staring out of windows when I could have been out traveling, learning, growing, *living*.

I determined to start living my life, then and there. I packed up and migrated to Taos, New Mexico, where I slept on the mesa in a house made of bottles and wind, and feasted every morning on sky and space and sage-scent. (At the same time, I supported my little sister's decision to quit high school.) I spent as much time as I could dancing.

I continued to read John Holt, but I eventually decided to teach anyway. After all, school was going to exist whether I wanted it to or not, and I figured I might as well jump in and make it the best experience I could. Anyway, I didn't know *how* to do anything that I wanted to do more. I still felt that public school was a horrendous institution, but I daydreamed about finding a private school that was humane and lively.

I found a position teaching seventh and eighth grade English at a small independent school in Colorado. I was thrilled. It believed firmly in experiential education – learning by *doing* – and my colleagues and the administrators were wonderful people: flexible, enthusiastic, imaginative, intelligent, funny and warm. With only 19 students, I'd have the chance to know each of them well. It seemed so different from public school that I looked forward to it with great excitement.

The year did go smoothly in most respects. However, I began to feel that this small school was not essentially healthier than ordinary public schools for most of its students. Naturally, they received more individual attention than they would have in public school, but some of them experienced an uglier flip side of that individual attention: we teachers seemed to see or otherwise find out nearly everything about students' lives and would then hound them endlessly about things that were none of our business – missing homework assignments, social conflicts, messy notebooks, etc. Even when we were not inclined to pry or push, students had little privacy, no way to escape our eyes.

Furthermore, this small, 'caring' and 'creative' school was fundamentally the same as any ordinary public school, because it controlled students' lives. It continually dictated to them how to use their time. So what if they were role-playing the lives of the early colonists instead of just reading the dry words of their American history textbook? These cute 'experiential' activities we teachers took pride in had the same effect any schoolwork does. They stole kids' time and energy, so that John-the-numbers-genius-and-artist had no time to build his geometric sculptures, so that Andy couldn't pursue his fascination with well-made knives and guns, so that Kris and Chris and Rick and Young didn't have enough time to read, so that Shira – a brilliant actress and talented musician – was threatened with having to drop out of her outstanding chorale group if she missed any homework assignments.

In some ways, in fact, it seemed *more* harmful than public school. Homework was excessive, leaving students little freedom even at home. Lots of parents expected the school to help turn their offspring into lawyers and 'successful executives', and the school catered to this image enough that it put tremendous pressure on kids.

But despite all this, I decided to stay with teaching, and I brainstormed ways to make my classroom as healthy as possible. I wanted to give my students as much freedom within the realm of language arts as I could, so I devised an independent study programme complete with an innovative 'All As' grading system borrowed from Richard E Koop of Gulf Middle School in Florida. The assistant headteacher, a courageous, warm woman, gave me her blessing, saying that since I obviously had the kids' needs and growth foremost in my mind, she'd support my experiment.

I began my second year of teaching with high hopes that soon plummeted. Four or five people who loved to write (enough to do so in their spare time and vacations) thrived in the programme. It gave them official time to do what they wanted to do anyway – write novels or collections of short stories or long long essays – rather than drain their energy with specific assignments of a specific length to fit into specific schedules. But most of my students saw it as just another way to make them do something they really didn't want or need to do, at least not every day. So much for freedom.

After I had felt dismal for a while because my curriculum hadn't dramatically changed the nature of school, we went on a week-long field trip to Washington, DC. Conflict was inevitable; the teachers who designed the trip naturally wanted to take as much advantage as possible of all the things to see and do in the area, so our schedule was hectic and demanding. At one point, the students were scolded for slouching and whispering during a dull evening lecture after a particularly exhausting day. As students exploded in their own defense, and one of my favorite students said sincerely that he wanted to go home, my mind reeled. It was perfectly fair, I thought, to expect people to behave wonderfully in any situation they chose freely to be part of. If I went to a film and talked all through it, I'd deserve to get kicked out. If I didn't feel like sitting quietly, I shouldn't go in the first place. But our students hadn't been given any choice as to whether they wanted to sit through a lecture, or even whether they went to Washington, or, for that matter, whether they sat in English and science every day.

That night I lay in bed agitating till 4am. Although I hadn't upbraided our students on that particular evening, I had certainly done so countless other times, for similar and sometimes less justifiable reasons.

I called Holt's writings up in my mind and admitted to myself that he was right – school was a bad place, a controlling place, and I wasn't going to change anything by being there. I could see that some of my students were fed up with school, but I knew they had no clue as to other possibilities. And so the seeds of this book sprouted in my brain. Also, in the back of my head I knew I could not continue to teach, but at first I refused to look this knowledge in the face. The prospect of life without my 'career' was frightening and uncertain. However, I started looking at the world with a fresher, more honest perspective. While bustling along the sidewalk and scolding students for dawdling, I thought longingly how I would enjoy spending a leisurely week in DC with a few of my students, talking with the homeless who camped opposite the White House, roaming the Smithsonian for days, taking time out for skateboarding and sky staring.

Back in Colorado, my convictions strengthened daily. I noticed an Emerson quote on the bulletin board, and I shivered: 'If you put a chain around the neck of a slave,' it said, 'the other end fastens itself around your own.' The final catalyst came the Friday I read Thoreau with my classes. Nearly everything he said seemed to pertain to the whole school issue, but one fragment in particular of 'On the Duty of Civil Disobedience' lodged itself in my brain. After explaining that he would not pay his taxes so long as they supported such evils as slavery, Thoreau had written:

> If any tax gatherer, or any other public officer, asks me, as one has done, 'But what shall I do?' my answer is, 'If you really wish to do anything, resign your office.' When the subject has refused allegiance, and the officer has resigned his office, then the revolution is accomplished.

That was that. Forced to face my own responsibility, I resolved first to give up teaching, and then to write this book. John Holt and a few others had written a stack of excellent books on unschooling, but I felt that teenagers needed their *own* book, one to tell them they weren't wrong to hate school, and to make them aware of alternatives.

The rest of the teaching year was horribly difficult and odd. In the classroom I vacillated between the easygoing, honest human being I wanted to be, and the businesslike teacher I knew I had to be if my class was to function. One day I'd sit laughing with my students, talking about a story one of them had written, ignoring their gum chewing (against school rules) or 'off-task' behavior. The next day I'd hand out detentions for swearing, lateness and of course any rude, sarcastic or otherwise 'inappropriate' statements. In my confused inconsistency, I imagine I was a more frightening authority figure than a military-style teacher would have been; sometimes it seemed that no sooner had students let down their guard and begun to think of me as a real person, than I would snap nervously back into teacher mode and bitch at them for 'disrupting'.

I could not tell my students about my raging opinions with a clear professional conscience, but I couldn't *not* tell them with a clear moral conscience. A friend sent me a button that said 'Free the Kids', and I wore it. Some days I was afraid that by writing I'd lose all my friends and even the trust of my students themselves. I finally told two students what I was up to, and of course had some guilty professional twangs about doing so. But I desperately hoped that I would finish, and that my book would find its way into my students' hands, in time for them to decide whether they wanted it to make a difference in their lives. June came; I hugged my students and colleagues goodbye amidst plenty of tears; I moved to Oregon and set up camp with my computer. Then, with a shiver and a grin, I hunkered down to write these pages for you.

HOW TO USE THIS BOOK

Notice that it's divided into four parts. The first tells why you should consider leaving school. The second tells how to get ready to do it. The third and fourth suggest ideas for what you can do once you've left. I have put it in the best order I could, but you can read it in any order you like.

I don't list a lot of specific resources in this edition; there's simply not room and, anyway, different resources are available in different countries, and each year new resources become available. I strongly recommend that you do get your hands on most or all of the tools listed in the Appendix, which will lead you to specific books, videos, programs and organizations, and other great helpers. It's also very important that you get comfortable seeking out your own resources, via the library, the Internet, magazines, conversations with mentors, etc. If you can't find something, ask the reference librarian.

When I mention ages of particular teenagers, I mean their ages at the time that they wrote to me or to *Growing Without Schooling* magazine (hereafter referred to as *GWS*). Some of the 15-year-olds are now 25.

There is a lot of information in your hands. Don't feel obliged to follow up on all of it, or most of it. Don't let it overwhelm you. Let it guide you to a few important things and let the rest go. The silences and spaces in your 'education' are as necessary as your activity.

On the other hand, this book does not tell everything that's possible. Don't be limited by my suggestions, just use them as starting points. I may revise this book again, eventually, so I'd welcome your recommendations for resources, or news of your own activities, or any other responses.

One more thing. All of us rise or sink to other people's expectations of us. Our society seems not to believe in teenagers enough to expect much of them. This book may shock you, therefore, when it tells how to plan a trip around the world, or when it suggests you start a business or become seriously involved in some academic field you love. But you're no imbecile, I'm certain, because at 15 I wasn't an imbecile. I didn't know much, but if the right information and some freedom had come my way, I could have soared. I hope that this book can provide some of that 'right information' for you, and that it helps you find the freedom you need.

Enjoy your flight … and tell me where you land.

PART 1 | Making the Decision

1 | Sweet Land of Liberty

How strange and self-defeating that supposedly free countries should train their young for life in totalitarianism.

No, David, wait until after class to use the bathroom.

Unfortunately, your daughter would rather entertain the class than participate appropriately.

Carter, if I have to ask you again to sit down, you'll be taking a trip to the office.

I'd love to hear what you have to say, Monty, but you need to raise your hand first.

Tonight you need to finish the exercises on page 193 and read the next section.

Marisa, I need a written explanation as to why you didn't give in your homework today.

What do you think of when you hear the word 'freedom'? The end of slavery? The fall of the Berlin Wall? A prisoner tunneling his way out of solitary confinement in Chile with a spoon? An old woman escaping her broken body in death? Gorillas dancing in the jungle instead of sulking behind bars? When I hear the word 'freedom', I remember the sweetest sunlight pouring over my teenaged cheeks on the first sleeping-in mornings of summer vacations.

Do you go to school? Yes? Then ...

... YOU ARE NOT FREE

The most overwhelming reality of school is *control*. School controls the way you spend your time (what is life made of if not time?), how you behave, what you read and to a large extent what you think. In school you can't control your own life. Outside school you can, at least to the extent that your parents trust you to. 'Comparing me to those who are conventionally schooled,' writes 12-year-old unschooler Colin Roch, 'Is like comparing the freedoms of a wild stallion to those of cattle in a feedlot' (*GWS* no. 78).

The ultimate goal of this book is for you to start associating the concept of freedom with *you*, and to start wondering why you and your friends don't have much of it, and for you to move out of the busy-prison into the meadows of life. There are lots of very good reasons to leave school but, to my idealistic American mind, the pursuit of freedom encompasses most of them and outshines the others.

If you look at the history of freedom, you notice that the most frightening thing about people who are not free is that they learn to take their bondage for granted, and to believe that this bondage is 'normal' and natural. They may not like it, but few question it or imagine anything different. There was a time when many black slaves took a sort of pride – or talked as if they took pride – in how well-behaved and hard-working they were. There was a time when most women believed – or talked as if they believed – that they should obey and submit to their husbands. In fact, people within an oppressed group often internalize their oppression so much that they are crueler, and more judgmental, to their peers than the oppressors themselves are. In China, men made deformed female feet into sexual fetishes, but it was the *women* who tied the cords on their own daughters' feet.

Obviously, black and female people eventually caught

sight of a greater vision for themselves, and change blazed through their minds, through laws, through public attitudes. All is not yet well, but the United States is now far kinder to people of color and with mammary glands than it was 100 years ago. What's more, these people are kinder to *themselves*. They dream bigger dreams, and flesh out grander lives, than picking cotton for the master or making a martini for the husband.

Right now, a lot of you are helping history to repeat itself; you don't believe you *should* be free. Of course you *want* to be free – in various ways, not just free of school. However, society gives you so many condescending, false and harmful messages about yourselves that most of you wouldn't trust yourselves with freedom. It's all complicated by the fact that the people who infringe most dangerously and inescapably on your freedom are often those who say they are helping you, those who are convinced you need their help: teachers, school counselors, perhaps your parents.

WHY *SHOULD* YOU HAVE FREEDOM?

Why should anyone? To become human, to live fully. Insofar as you live what someone else dictates, you do not live. Choice is a fundamental essence of life, and in the fullest life, each choice is deliberate and savored.

Another reason you should be free is obvious. You need to learn to live responsibly and joyfully in a free country.

Recently, schoolpeople have begun to talk a lot about 'experiential education'. Educators have wisely realized that the best way to teach anything includes not only reading about a subject, but also practicing it. For example, my colleague Gary Oakley taught science by having students rehabilitate a polluted pond. Naturally, what you learn this way sinks in more deeply than what you do by merely reading, hearing lectures and discussing. It means participating – *being* a scientist or musician rather than watching from the outside.

What the educators apparently haven't realized yet is that experiential education is a double-edged sword. If you do something to learn it, then what you do, you learn. All the time you are in school, you learn through experience how to live in a dictatorship. In school you shut your notebook when the bell rings. You do not speak unless granted permission. You are guilty until proven innocent, and who will prove you innocent? You are told what to do, think and say for six hours each day. If your teacher says sit up and pay attention, you had better stiffen your spine and try to get Bobby or Sally or the idea of spring or the play you're writing off your mind. The most constant and thorough thing students in school experience – and learn – is the antithesis of democracy.

When I was in sixth grade, I had the good fortune to learn that democracy outside school is not a crime, at the same time that I learned (not for the first time) that democracy in schools is a crime. Two of my friends and I were disgusted by the state of our school lunches. After finding mold on the rolls one day and being generally fed up with the cardboard taste of things, we decided to take action. Stephanie and Stacey started a petition. Its purpose was a bit misspelled and unclear, but at the top it said something that meant, 'Sign below if you are tired of revolting lunches, and put a mark by your name if your roll was mouldy on Tuesday'. People signed the petition during lunch; we had three pages or so of sloppy signatures on wrinkly notebook paper.

Apparently some teachers got wind of what we were up to, and Miss Petersen (fake name) told Stephanie to give her the petition. After Miss Petersen looked at it sternly, she said she'd have to turn it over to the principal. Stephanie and I panicked. We held a secret meeting that afternoon in the hills and looked at each other with sick scared faces. We tried to convince ourselves that young criminals got off easily.

The next day Miss Petersen was moving a piano down the hall. Our brave friend Kelly walked by in his line on the way in from lunch. He saw the petition sitting on the piano, and he snatched it up. Miss Petersen didn't see him. He returned the petition to me. Go, team.

Stephanie and Stacey were summoned to the principal. He demanded to have the petition back, but since they didn't yet know about its recovery, they said earnestly that Miss Petersen had it. He lectured them on their disrespect for authority, and said there was nothing wrong with the lunches, and that he didn't want to *ever* hear anything about petitions again, was that clear?

I took out my sky-blue stationery with the mushrooms on it and wrote a letter to the governor. I apologized for not typing and for the wrinkliness and bad spelling of the petition. Then I explained why it was important that our lunches improve. I didn't say anything about the trouble we were in at school; I didn't want him to know how bad we were. I looked him up in the phone book, got his address and sent it off. I was afraid he would report me to the principal, but I was ready to sacrifice myself for the cause.

The week after the end of the term, my father brought the post in with a strange face. 'Grace,' he said, 'Are you personally acquainted with Cecil Andrus?'

I tore the letter open. The governor said not to worry about my handwriting, that he would have responded sooner had I sent the letter to his office instead of his house, and that he sympathized with my plight. He told me that school lunches weren't in his control, but he gave me the address of the people who could make a difference. Best – and most surprising – of all, he congratulated me on my 'good citizenship' and encouraged me to keep on speaking up when something wasn't right in the world. During the next six years, the memory of that experience often helped me keep my hope and sanity while my friends and I were silenced, subtly and blatantly, again and again, by 'authority'.

Ah, yes ...

... AUTHORITY

Regardless of what the law or your teachers have to say about this, you are as human as anyone over the age of 18 or 21, yet, 'minors' are one of the most oppressed groups of people in the world, and certainly the most discriminated against legally.

It starts at home. Essentially, your parents can require you to do almost anything and forbid you to do almost anything. Fortunately, most parents try hard not to abuse this power. Yet, from a legal standpoint, the reason schools have so much tyrannical power over you is that they act in *loco parentis* – in place of the parent. As legal parental substitutes, they can search your locker or bag, tell you to be quiet, read your post (notes), speak rudely to you and commit other atrocities – things I hope your parents would not do with a clean conscience, and things no sensible adult would do to another adult, for fear of losing a job or ending a friendship.

Many teenagers, of course, do clash with their parents to some extent. But most parents like and love their children enough to listen to their side, grant them more freedom as they grow, back off when they realize they're overbearing and generally be reasonable. The schools may do this with some 'rebellious' students, but not usually, and not after a second or third 'offense'. Schools are too big, and the adults in them too overworked, to see 'rebels' as people – instead, such students get a permanent-ink 'bad person' label and unreasonable treatment. Even in a small private school, authority is often unyielding and unfairly judgmental.

When I was substitute teaching in Oakland, California, one day they told me I could have a month-long job teaching choir and piano while the regular teacher had a baby. As it happened, I did have a fairly substantial musical background and could have handled at least that aspect of the job easily. But the administrators showed no interest in my musical knowledge – all they wanted was someone who could maintain order for a month. When the principal introduced me to the choir class, one of the students raised his hand and asked, 'Since she's not a music teacher, what are we supposed to do if she's not any good?'

The principal launched into a tirade about how it doesn't matter what you think of her teaching, you'll do exactly what she says and I don't want to hear about any problems from any of you; the state board of education decided she was good enough to be certified and that's all you need to know.

One of the worst things about this sort of arbitrary authority is it makes us lose our trust in natural authority – people who know what they're doing and could share a lot of wisdom with us. When they make you obey the cruel and unreasonable teacher, they steal your desire to learn from the kind and reasonable teacher. When they tell you to be sure to clear up after yourselves in the cafeteria, they steal your own natural sense of courtesy.

Many times, I have heard teachers resort defiantly to the proclamation that 'The bottom line is, they need to do what we tell them because they're the kids and we're the adults'. This concept that teenagers should obey simply because of their age no longer makes any sense to me. I can't work out what it is based on, except adults' own egos. In this regard, school often seems like a circus arena full of authority-craving adults. Like trained animals, you are there to make them look good, to help them believe that they are better than you.

But maybe you're not yet convinced. The sudden proclamation that you deserve to be free sounds too glib, too easy. Let's turn the question upside down.

ARE THERE ANY GOOD REASONS YOU *SHOULDN'T* HAVE FREEDOM?

Since schools supposedly exist to help you learn, the only legitimate answer they could offer is that you have to sacrifice freedom for the sake of learning. If learning and freedom were incompatible, having to choose would be tragic. But learning is *not* dependent upon school or upon slavery. If this doesn't strike you as obvious, I hope it will by the time you've finished reading the next chapter.

A wise friend of mine, who grew up in Germany under Hitler and later did time in American prison camps, startled me with a different reason you shouldn't have freedom. First, he agreed that schools are the antithesis of freedom. Then he said, but how can you really appreciate the freedom that comes with adulthood in a democracy, if you never know what it's like to live without it? I thought a lot about what he said, but I ended up deciding that a 12-year experiential lesson in bondage doesn't make freedom seem precious; it makes it seem impossible. It also misrepresents the nature of learning. After school, too many people continue to slap chains on themselves. Before school, few people are so self-hating. Maybe after we abolish compulsory schooling in the 21st century we can set up voluntary month-long camps where people sit at desks and obey, just so they realize how lucky they are not to live their lives that way, just so they promise themselves to always live in celebration of their freedom.

Maybe you believe you aren't ready for freedom?

On some level, no one ever is; it's not a matter of age. People of all ages make mistakes with their freedom –

becoming involved with destructive friends, choosing to study subjects they're not deeply interested in, buying houses with rotten foundations, clearcutting forests, breaking good marriages for stupid reasons. People cause tremendous pain and disaster, and you will never be so wise or perfect that you won't do stupid things. Sure, teenagers make mistakes. So do adults, and it seems to me adults have a harder time admitting and fixing theirs. While you are young, perhaps you are more likely to break your arm falling off a horse, but you are less likely to cause an oil spill or start a useless war. The only alternative to making mistakes is for someone to make all your decisions for you, in which case you will make their mistakes instead of your own. Obviously, that's not a life of integrity. So why not start living, rather than merely obeying, before the age of 18?

Part of my work in writing this book involved contacting all the unschooled teenagers I could find. I asked them each, as part of a questionnaire, what they considered the greatest advantages of unschooling. Almost unanimously, they agreed: *freedom!* Here are some typical comments:

You can spend your time and energy doing things you like.

I don't have to raise my hand to speak.

Not being forced to do certain uninteresting subjects. Not sitting around for six hours doing something I don't like.

Having time to do what I want.

[In school] you had to have *permission* to go to the bathroom!

I feel sorry for the kids who have to go to 'prison' for 6–8 hours a day. I felt like we were the victims of a mass production enterprise.

We are able to do so many things (go to the zoo, ride bikes, etc, etc) while other kids are just sitting in classes and desks being bored .... [One reason this unschooler's sane parents kept her out of school was they 'didn't like the idea of kids staying inside on sunny days.']

Time, time, time. I have my life back for my own use. I am no longer having to wait and wait and wait for everyone else. I can concentrate on what I want to learn. I can work on my computer as long as I like. Or if I want to spend a lot of time diagramming sentences one day and not at all for two days, it's all right. Also we can travel and be in general control our own lives! It's great!

I'm *free*!

2 | School is Not for Learning

My schooling not only failed to teach me what it professed to be teaching, but prevented me from being educated to an extent which infuriates me when I think of all I might have learned at home by myself.

George Bernard Shaw, *Everybody's Political What's What*

Schools and schooling are increasingly irrelevant to the great enterprises of the planet. No one believes any more that scientists are trained in science classes or politicians in civics classes or poets in English classes. The truth is that schools don't really teach anything except how to obey orders.

John Taylor Gatto, New York State Teacher of the Year 1991[1]

The consensus is overwhelming. After dozens of nearly identical, predictable conversations with friends and acquaintances, I'm no longer certain this chapter is necessary.

'Do you think you learned a lot at school?' I'd ask.

'Oh no, of course not,' came the typical reply, 'I mean, I memorized a lot of facts for tests, but I don't remember any of it except a few things I was really interested in.'

The unschooled teenagers who responded to my questionnaire offered similar comments. 'The one thing I didn't do at school,' wrote Jason Lescalleet, 14, 'was learn.'

Indeed, many of these teenagers had given up school because of 'lack of learning' or intellectual boredom.

Once out of school, things improved. I asked unschooled teens how they would rate their 'academic' knowledge and skills in comparison to that of their schooled peers. Most of them felt like Kevin Sellstrom, 14, who said, 'Far superior. More knowledgeable in most subjects, including common sense.'

Many teenagers angrily complained that school had wasted their time. 'Without it,' they said, 'you learn more in less time.' Jason Lescalleet says that out of school 'I get to learn instead of sitting with my head down.' This common sense we all seem to share – that people don't need school to learn – is proved in a more academic and official way by the work of Dr Brian Ray's *Home School Researcher*. Ray and other researchers have shown that homeschoolers' academic test scores are consistently higher than school students'.[2]

WHY DON'T PEOPLE LEARN IN SCHOOL?

The most basic and overwhelming reason shoots us right back into the last chapter. Our brains and spirits are the freest things in the universe. Our bodies can live in chains, but our intellects cannot. It's that simple. The mind *will* be free, or it will be dead. It can be numbed, quieted and restrained so that it memorizes names of Portuguese explorers and plods through grades one to twelve. If it is fiercely alive and teamed up with a forgiving spirit, it may find a way to be free even in school, and stay awake that way. But these activities are defenses, not full-fledged learning.

There are other reasons school prevents learning too – fear of 'bad' grades, lack of faith in one's abilities (usually due to previous unpleasant experiences with grades – including A minuses), an occasional uninformed teacher, illogical or inherently dull teaching methods and books, lack of individual attention, oxygen-starved classrooms.

These problems are the ones the educators can see. They

exhaust themselves seeking solutions – hiring the brightest teachers they can get, searching the ends of the earth for easier ways to learn spelling, providing counseling services, buying textbooks with technicolor photographs, working hard on 'anticipatory sets' (the beginning part of lessons which are supposed to 'grab students' attention). Most of these educators – especially when they are teachers rather than superintendents of school boards – do some good. If lots of people continue to go to school, I hope that the idealistic educators continue their efforts. These efforts make school more pleasant, the same way that clean sheets and warm blankets make a prison more pleasant than do bare scratchy mattresses with thin covers.

Their efforts cannot, however, make you free. Even if they encourage you to write research papers on topics that interest you, even if they reduce the amount of homework they assign, they cannot encourage you to follow joyfully your own intellectual mysteries, except in your spare time after your homework. To do so would be to undermine completely the basic structure of the schools.

Because they can never make you free, schools can never allow you to learn fully.

LOVE OF LEARNING

If you had always been free to learn, you would follow your natural tendency to find out as fully as possible about the things that interest you, cars or stars. We are all born with what they call 'love of learning', but it dives off into an elusive void when we go to school.

After all, school does not help you focus on what you love, because it insists that you devote equal time to six or so 'subjects.' While interviewing an unschooled actress for *GWS* (no. 73), editor Susannah Sheffer made an astute observation: 'It's funny that people think kids should be well rounded but don't seem to have the same expectations of adults. Adults seem to realize you can't do everything.' In *Walden*, Thoreau laments, 'Our lives are frittered away by detail,' and admonishes, 'Simplicity, simplicity, simplicity! I say, let your affairs be as two or three, and not a hundred or a thousand.'

Of course, quitting school doesn't guarantee that you are going to learn more in *every* subject than you did in school. If you hate geography at school, and decide to continue studying it outside school, it's possible that you won't enjoy it any more or learn it much better, although being able to work without ridicule at your own speed will help. You *will* see a dramatically wonderful change in the way you learn about the things that interest you. What's more, you will find out that you are interested in things that haven't yet caught your attention, and that you can love at least some of the things which repulsed you at school.

Beyond the love and pursuit of something specific, there's another quality you might also call love of learning. It's simple curiosity, which kills more tired assumptions than cats. Some people move around with their ears and eyes wide open like raccoons, ready to find out something new and like it. Do everything you can to cultivate this characteristic; it will enliven your life immeasurably.

However, curiosity is another stubborn quality that thrives on freedom; therefore, school squishes it. Curiosity is an active habit – it needs the freedom to explore and move around and get your hands into lots of pots. It needs the freedom to watch TV with the remote control and flip through the channels at will. It needs the freedom to thumb through *Science News* and stop only where you want to. It needs the freedom to browse through your library's whole shelf of poetry.

Curiosity puts itself on hold when it isn't allowed to move at its own pace. I am thinking of the week-long field trip our middle school took to Washington, DC, and of how my own curiosity took a nap during most of our guided tours, even at the 'fun' places like Williamsburg and Jamestown, and how I raced around excitedly when we had an unleashed day at the Smithsonian.

On the up side, the ironic truth is that everyone loves to learn – or at least did as a baby, and can get to be that way again. As John Holt points out, 'Children do not need to be made to learn about the world, or shown how. They want to, and they know how.' In fact, it could all add up to a great opening line the night you decide to break the news to your parents: 'Mum, Dad, I'd really like to leave school because I'd rather learn.'

REPORT CARDS VERSUS FREEDOM

Schools do have a few poor-quality substitutes for freedom. They know that if you dry up people's love for learning, you will certainly dry up their learning itself, unless you come through with a handy replacement: pressure; threats; bribes; tests; As, Bs, Cs, Ds and Fs. Yes, indeed, school does have one way to make you learn that you might not easily duplicate in a free life. Without an exam on Friday, maybe you wouldn't learn how to solve differential equations. Without a 25-dollar prize from your parents, maybe you wouldn't memorize the periodic table in order to get an A in chemistry. Maybe the pressure of grades and all the expectant hoopla and significance surrounding them *does* help you to learn more.

Temporarily.

The day after the test, or the week after school's finished, will you even take time to kiss your fact collection goodbye as it floats off on the breeze? In the long run, pressure is an ineffective substitute for curiosity and the freedom to pursue those things you love, because people only remember and think about things they use or care about.

A lot of teachers believe learning depends on grades, because they are only used to seeing education take place in the forced environment of school. Physicist Frank Oppenheimer had a clearer head, putting massive energy into non-school learning environments (For example, he started the Exploratorium, an innovative museum in San Fransisco). About learning without grades, he said, 'People built fires to keep warm long before Galileo invented the thermometer.'[3]

Furthermore, the emphasis schools put on grades *prevents* healthy learning, even if it coaxes you into quickie learning.

REPORT CARDS VERSUS LEARNING

Bad grades start a vicious circle. They make you feel like a failure. A sense of failure cripples you and *prevents* you from succeeding. Therefore, you continue to get bad grades and continue to be stifled. Of course, bad grades are relative – in many families Bs are bad grades, especially if the Firstborn Son did better or Uncle Harold went to Yale. Feeling like a failure is a self-fulfilling prophecy, which is why most school dropouts make statistics that the schoolpeople love to quote. Think about it. Would you continue to enjoy (and improve at) skateboarding or hiking if someone scrutinized your every move, reported to your parents, and acted as if you'd never succeed in life if you didn't perfect your double kick flip before Friday, or add ten pounds to your pack and reach the pass by noon?

Obviously, we all need both privacy and respect to enjoy (learn) any activity. By privacy, I don't mean solitude. I mean freedom from people poking their noses into your business or 'progress'.

People assume that grades tell how intelligent you are, but of course they don't. They mostly reflect how well you co-operated by doing what your teachers said. They also reflect whether your teachers like or know you. Bad grades don't mean you can't read, write or think. Good grades don't show whether you can find out how to do something you believe in and then follow through and do it. They don't show the most fundamental aspect of intelligence – whether you learn from your experiences and 'mistakes.' They don't show whether you live with courage, compassion, curiosity or common sense. Even in an objective scientific sense, grades and exam results are not accurate measurements of your intelligence.

The world and its complex, terrible, wonderful webs of civilization are far bigger and older than our 19th-century factory-style compulsory schooling system. There is room for all kinds of people – those who love books, and those who'd rather build things and take them apart all day, not just for an hour in the woodshop or autoshop. There is room for those who would rather wander dreaming on a glacier, and perhaps awaken the rest of us with some truthful words in the tradition of Gilbert White, Henry David Thoreau, Ed Abbey, Annie Dillard and Barry Lopez. There is room for those who want to make lasagne and homemade French bread and apple pie all day. None of these callings is better or worse than others. None means failure as a human being, but they may cause failure in a dull system that you never asked to be a part of in the first place.

Furthermore, bad grades and other consequences of not doing your 'work' punish you for what you *do* do (making friends, reading extracurricular novels) as much as for what you don't do. Tell me why, if you want to spend two days following badger tracks, you should be penalized for your choice with zeros in five or six subjects and a truancy to boot.

Good grades are often equally dangerous. They encourage you to forsake everything worthwhile that you might love, just to keep getting them. When schoolpeople give you good grades, you give them your unquestioning loyalty in return. It makes me think of the Algonkian Indians who gave Manhattan Island to the Dutch in exchange for six dollars' worth of trinkets. We are not talking here about fair bargains; we are talking about manipulation and colossal rip-off.

Good grades, moreover, are addictive. You start to depend on them for your sense of self-worth, and then it becomes nearly impossible to do anything that will jeopardize them. When you have good grades, you have something to lose, and so you stop taking risks. The best things in life come from taking risks. My little sister, who is more intelligent than I am, always got bad grades. She also has an easier time being honest and direct with people than I do. I think these two bits of data are closely connected. The system never gave her any gold stars, so she didn't feel obliged to give it any soft, false, silent agreement in return. (On the other hand, she ended up with plenty of unnecessary failure-complex to work through.)

Finally, grades confuse the meaning of education. Patrick Meehan, a 14-year-old unschooler, told me, 'Giving grades puts the wrong focus on learning. It points a student toward competition and learning for the wrong reasons: to make grades rather than to become educated.'

SOME MORE WAYS THAT SCHOOLS PREVENT PEOPLE FROM LEARNING

Schools require passivity. When I taught English and history, I learned far more about them than I ever had in school and – in some ways – even in college. That's because teaching is an active role: seeking out and selecting readings, designing assignments, evaluating others' work. Sitting and doing those assignments and receiving those grades is the bottom of the learning ladder.

Schools cram you too full too fast. I don't mean they challenge you. I mean they throw too much busywork in your face. Being in school is like being incredibly hungry and sitting at Burger King eating too much, too fast to be satisfied, and then puking it up. Good learning, like good eating, is not only mental and physical, but also spiritual. Generally, you can satisfy the craving only in calm. If you don't have sufficient time or peace to digest knowledge, it only gives you a headache.

Schoolpeople care more about appearances than about learning. Just before a field trip, an administrator I worked with talked to students about 'expectations'. 'We just want you to look nice,' she said, 'that's the most important thing.' I don't think she heard herself, or quite meant to say that, but I couldn't forget it – as it says in the Bible, the mouth speaks what the heart is full of. In my own classroom, I harped on the way students sat. It didn't matter how well they could concentrate curled up on the couch, I was petrified that another adult would walk in and decide I was Incompetent. So most days students sat with their feet flat on the floor, stiff spined and uncomfortable.

School isn't challenging enough if you're academically inclined. It's not merely that school is too easy; you are not necessarily a straight-A student and in fact may feel overwhelmed by piles of homework. But so much of it is busywork with no connection to the molten cores of physics, mythology, philosophy. It also doesn't help that most of your fellow students would rather *not* be reading Milton.

Schools present learning backwards, emphasizing answers instead of questions. Answers are dead ends, even when they're 'correct'. Questions open the galaxies.

School asks you to wear yourself out attaining mediocrity in six or so subjects rather than be amazing at one or two you love. Some schools and educators do believe in cultivating a student's uniqueness but, without major structural changes, they can't. As long as focusing on algebra means you get a C in psychology, or as long as you get lectured for falling asleep in history on mornings after late gymnastics sessions, you are being pushed away from excellence toward anxious shoddiness.

School won't answer the door when real chances to learn come knocking. There's nothing wrong with planning and setting goals – they help us to accomplish big things like writing books or pulling off a bike trip across Turkey. But life is unexpected. Sometimes it offers us something more glorious than what we'd planned, and we lose out if we're not ready to let go of our agenda. Christians call it surrendering to the will of God. Eastern mystics call it letting go of ego, going with the flow. Whatever you call it, school has little room for it.

For example: on our middle school field trip to Washington, DC, our self-imposed schedule demanded that we visit the Capitol for a predetermined length of time and then proceed directly to the next attraction. This schedule left no time for what might happen on the way into the Capitol. What did happen was that on the steps five students and two teachers stopped to talk to a Vietnam veteran fasting for US reconciliation with Vietnam. He'd swallowed nothing but juice for 70 days. We listened to him with awe. At one point he asked, 'Do you know what constitutional amendment guarantees me the right to sit here and talk about this?' Young, who always had the answers to all the questions, said, 'The first!'

'Very good,' pronounced another teacher, who at that moment had arrived on the scene. We all jumped. What did 'very good' have to do with anything? She continued: 'And which amendment prohibited slavery?' 'The thirteenth,' answered Young. 'Exactly! And with that, let's be on our way,' suggested our chaperone brightly. The rest of us looked at each other in vague incredulity; the disruption of learning was more awkwardly obvious than usual. Then we trudged up the steps behind her.

(By the way, this event is also a perfect example of the way teachers and administrators are not allowed to be themselves in school, being required instead to fulfill ridiculous authoritarian roles. The woman who interrupted us was as curious and human as any of the rest of us, but at that moment she felt a particularly strong responsibility to keep us on schedule. Later she told me she wished she could have encouraged a longer conversation. I understood her position exactly, thinking of all the times I'd told students to come away from the window and sit at their tables, knowing that whatever they saw or dreamed of out of the window was more important than writing a short story they didn't want to write.)

In general, school screens us off from reality – no matter how we define reality. Is reality in books, in the intellect? If it is, school censors more than it reveals. Does reality lurk in raw adventure? In religion? In culture? In friendship and community? In work? If so, school just gets in the way.

Not only does your actual time in school block out learning, but it also prevents you from learning outside school. It drains your time and energy. After you have written your descriptive essay and reviewed your Spanish verbs, it's time for bed, so how are you supposed to think or write the poem you were imagining in history? How are you supposed to find the energy to go outside and admire the unfolding buds on the oak tree?

School wouldn't be nearly so oppressive if it didn't demand center stage in your life. More times than I can count, I've heard adults tell teenagers, with appalling arrogance, that if they don't start getting their homework in on time, they'll have to stop drama, or choir, or hockey, or their job, or spending the night at friends' houses, or whatever it is that they love. Imagine a concert pianist getting ready for a performance. As she throws on her coat, her husband blocks the doorway. 'Oh, honey,' he says, 'I'm afraid I can't let you go. You haven't prepared next week's menus, and you've left the music room in a mess. Until you get your priorities straight, you'll just have to stay at home.'

Finally, schools play a nasty trick on all of us. *They make learning so unpleasant and frightening* that they scare many people away from countless pleasures: evenings browsing in libraries, taking an edible plants walk at the nature center, maybe even working out trigonometry problems for the hard beauty and challenge of it. Luckily (and ironically), many things we learn from are not called 'learning experiences' by schools, so we don't attach that schoolish learning stigma to them. But by calling school 'learning', schools make learning sound like an excruciatingly boring way to waste a nice afternoon. That's sad.

'Well', perhaps I hear you say, 'indeed I do not learn much at school, but I *do* learn a little. *If I leave, I won't learn* anything.'

Forgive my rudeness, but that's upside-down thinking. As John Holt said, if it's the medicine that makes you sick, more medicine will just make you sicker. And if you stop taking it, you'll get well.

You wouldn't suggest that you can't learn without school, if school hadn't crushed your faith in yourself in the first place. Before you went to school, you taught yourself to speak. After you leave school, you will teach yourself how to live on your own and how to find out answers to questions that interest you. Even now, you learn on your own every time you do anything of your own free will – kicking a soccer ball, falling in love, playing on computers, riding horses, reading books, thinking, disobeying rules.

In school, too, you already teach yourself; you just do it in the company of people who take the credit for your progress. I talk a lot with my brother Ned about education. He got marvelous grades at school, won a city-wide contest sponsored by Hewlett-Packard, and went on to get a degree in electrical engineering. He learned at school, he says, because of the reading he did and the questions he thought about. Teachers had little to do with it. If the laboratory equipment and other resources at school had been high quality, that would have helped immensely – but they weren't, so they didn't. He was at school, but he taught himself. And he learned more at home, on his own – building a computer, taking things apart, messing around.

Yes, when your teacher talks he shares his knowledge, which may be high-quality fascinating knowledge or low-quality dull knowledge. But your teacher cannot bridge the gap between what you know and what you want to know. For his words to 'educate' you, you must welcome them, think about them, find somewhere in your mind to organize them and remember them. Your learning is your job, not your teachers' job. And all you need to start with is desire. You *don't* need a schoolteacher to get knowledge – you can get it from looking at the world, from reading, from watching films, from conversations, from asking questions, from experience. As John Holt says in *GWS* no. 40, 'The most important thing any teacher has to learn, not to be learned in any school of education I ever heard of, can be expressed in seven words: *learning is not the product of teaching*. Learning is the product of the activity of learners …'

In fact, in today's information-laden USA, anyone who has acquired basic skills in reading, writing and maths computation can learn nearly anything they want to, on their own. Books, libraries, generous and knowledgeable people, the Internet and other resources make this possible. Young or old, anyone can in fact become an expert in a field they love, if they are not restrained and occupied by the petty nonsense of school or meaningless work. Part of learning is often contacting and receiving help from others, but learning does not require a boss, a rigid schedule, a schoolroom, or most of the other things schools provide.

Nor does it require a whip. Until school destroys the joy and naturalness of learning, young children revel wide-eyed in the intricacies of their world, learning to talk without teachers, asking questions, growing.

'Well, but what about all the things school has to make me learn?' What about them? The good things schools have are equipment and teachers. The bad things they have are schedules, grades, compulsory attendance, authority, dull textbooks, busywork, sterile atmospheres, too much homework, and teachers. You do not need to go to school to have teachers (or helpers, tutors, mentors) or equipment. If you want schoolteachers and equipment without school, maybe you can organize it. *See* chapter 16.

'But what about all the mysterious techniques and scientific approaches they use to make me learn? Don't teachers know a lot more than I do about learning?' Not at all. Most teachers know about classroom management – how to threaten, manipulate or cajole a class into quietly doing its work. Many can explain things clearly. Some even overflow with true enthusiasm for their subject, so that a few students are infected with a love of that same subject. All this, however, is a sorry substitute for the recognition that you have a mind of your own and are capable of using it. Teachers would be infinitely more helpful if they knew a lot and cheerfully answered questions, dispensed wisdom and pointed out resources – but only when you asked them to.

As for all those mysterious techniques – relax. Nothing happens in school that can't happen elsewhere, and in fact most of what happens there is nothing but a shadow of real world learning. After all, nothing complicated takes place at school. In order to 'learn', you are made to read, write and receive criticism on written work, do other exercises and have them corrected, listen to a teacher talk, discuss ideas or information with teachers or with classmates under teacher supervision, conduct laboratory experiments, receive individual attention and 'do' things, fashionably called 'experiential education'. Almost all these school things you can do on your own. Substitute 'wise adult' for 'teacher', and you don't need school for *any* of them. School did not invent these activities and does not own them; they can be found outside school in much fresher, juicier form. Schools have no monopoly on learning, or even on 'school' methods of learning.

In the end, the secret to learning is so simple: forget about it. Think only about whatever you love. Follow it, do it, dream about it. One day, you will glance up at your collection of Japanese literature, or trip over the solar oven you built, and it will hit you: learning was there all the time, happening by itself.

3 | What School *Is* For

If schools get in the way of learning, why do we have them? Why did anyone ever think they would work?

Compulsory schooling in the US started because of some lofty, beautiful hopes for democracy, unfortunately mixed up with a lethal dose of arrogance and tainted with a few other impurities. Thomas Jefferson, John Adams and other early American leaders argued that in a democracy people needed to have knowledge and wisdom in order to make decent decisions together. Also, they hoped America could be a country where 'everyone' (meaning all the white boys who hadn't immigrated too recently) had an equal chance to succeed. Thus, they all needed a chance to learn and read and grow as children, rather than be packed off to factories for hard labor and be shut off from the world of books and ideas.

People hadn't always thought this way; in most of the old kingdoms of Europe, no one particularly wanted Johnny to learn to read, because Johnny's purpose in life was to herd cows and do what the king said. In England, compulsory school for poor people had started in the 15th century, but not in support of democracy. Instead, the idea was to train the destitute for jobs so that rich people wouldn't have to support them with tax money.[4]

In other words, the ideals that led to American public education were idealistic and revolutionary ones. How wonderful if the people who held them could have been democratic enough to trust and allow others to make the most of such an opportunity.

If so, we might have had one bonanza extravaganza of an educational system, one in which children were legally guaranteed their basic material needs – shelter and food – until a certain age – 16, 18, 22, whatever – and allowed to explore freely the physical and cultural worlds. Libraries and books could have been accessible to all. Tutors and academic specialists could have been paid by the government to answer people's questions, to teach students more intensively when they wanted that. Apprenticeships could have been available, as well as open laboratories staffed by scientists ready to let young people assist in their research. Children and teenagers could have roamed around sticking their hands into frog ponds, bread dough and art supplies. They could have invented gadgets, cataloged fossils and written poetry at will.

Instead, the people who thought up American education believed in no one but themselves. They did not trust children to learn, and they did not trust the 'lower classes' to want their children to learn. I doubt any kind of intellectual freedom even occurred to them. They believed that in order to have education, it would have to be forced. Thus came compulsory schooling. They modeled the American system on the German one, which never pretended and was not intended to create a democracy.

Another reason we have schools even though they prevent learning is that schools are intended not only for learning. They have other purposes too, somewhat less charming.

Although compulsory schooling was begun partly in hopes of educating people worthy of democracy, other goals also imbedded themselves in the educational system. One was the goal of creating obedient factory workers who did not waste time by talking to each other or daydreaming. Historian Lawrence A Cremin writes, '… There was one educational problem that proved ubiquitous wherever factories did appear, and that was the problem of nurturing and maintaining industrial discipline.' Cremin goes on to explain that before the industrial revolution, people had scheduled their lives in harmony with the seasons, holidays and their own preferences. But factories

> required a shift from agricultural time to the much more precise categories of industrial time, with its sharply delineated and periodized work day. Moreover, along with this shift in timing and rhythm, the factory demanded concomitant shifts in habits of attention and behavior, under which workers could no longer act according to whim or preference but were required instead to adjust to the needs of the productive process and the other workers involved in it ... The schools taught [factory behavior], not only through textbook preachments, but also through the very character of their organization – the grouping, periodizing, and objective impersonality were not unlike those of the factory.[5]

This industrial indoctrination continues full force in schools today, turning out people who conveniently obey authority, don't think too much, and work hard for little reward. Yet, as we hurtle into the information age, it makes even less sense for people to spend 12 years training for factory work.

When schools started educating everyone – girls and new immigrants, and in the US Native Americans, as well as white boys – they took on another purpose. Schools took on the task of stamping out 'minority' and other differing cultures. 'The Indian schools were like jails and run along military lines, with roll calls four times a day,' says Sioux medicine man Lame Deer in *Lame Deer, Seeker of Visions*.

Schools also exist to provide babysitting: preventing teenagers from competing in the job market or running loose in the streets. Like other school purposes, this goal stands smack in the way of learning; it translates mainly into an unforgivable waste of time. If we could scrap it, school could surely teach everything more efficiently, not 'reviewing' year after year, and you'd finish in half the time. When adults go to classes, there is usually little of the

educational hanky-panky and muddle and time wasting
you get in school. Unschooler Jessica Franz, 12, wrote to me,
'I feel that I am about at the same level as the kids at my
grade although I do "school" only occasionally as opposed
to six or seven hours a day.' Her comment is echoed by the
experiences of thousands of other unschoolers who spend
little formal time on academic tasks but know much much
more, and get better scores on standardized tests than the
average schooled student.

Contrast school's use of time with the way people study
for the US General Equivalency Diploma (GED). When
high school dropouts want to take it, they are typically
coached for 16 to 24 hours in total over a period of four to
six weeks. Books that prepare people to take the GED
suggest around 30 home-study sessions, each lasting about
one to three hours. That's all they need, *not* four years
sitting at a desk with someone else's bubble gum stuck
underneath.

I am reminded of a conversation my colleagues and I had
with a parent when I was teaching. We had suggested that
this man's son skip the eighth grade and go directly into the
ninth, since he was extremely bright, competent, socially
adept and 'responsible' in doing his schoolwork. At first,
the father had some qualms. He was worried that his son
would miss some of the 'building blocks' of courses such as
algebra, science and foreign languages. No, said the
teachers, Jasper (fake name) would miss nothing important
by skipping a grade.

That information was good for Jasper, since he was
allowed to skip eighth grade and save himself a year of
'nothing important'. But the implications of that
conversation are horrendous. Year after year, you attend
school for many reasons. You may think the most important
reason is learning, but in reality you are receiving 'nothing
important' in exchange for your 12 years of drudgery. Of
course, schools teach some potentially helpful skills and

information. But the amount of good stuff is insignificant next to the piles of inanity and, furthermore, the meat of most year-long courses could be covered in a good two- or three-day session.

Schools didn't begin in order to provide millions of jobs for teachers, administrators, maintenance people and office workers, but since they provide those jobs now, that is one of their main purposes. It is probably the one that will kick hardest if lots of young people leave. Yes, it would be tragic for all those people to be out of work. But why must you provide their livelihood with the skin of your soul? The government pays them to do dirty work; it might as well pay them to do good work – help in libraries and museums, provide teaching and tutoring to people of all ages who ask for it, read to blind and elderly people. In the meantime, it shouldn't be your burden.

Why do we stand for it? Why do most people believe unquestioningly in compulsory education? Because they are mystified, shamed and intimidated into believing in it, that's why. Schoolpeople often talk in a specialized, complicated language, as if learning were a specialized, complicated process. 'Mastery learning,' they say. 'Criterion-referenced testing, multicultural education, prosocial behavior, expository teaching and stanine scores. So there.' They pretend – and believe – that what they do is all very tricky and difficult.

Teachers take themselves very seriously when they do things like design courses and lesson plans. They try to sound very scientific when speaking to students and talking about students. (Remember, I know because I was a teacher. I didn't just see it, I did it. It's a tremendously addictive power trip.)

Indeed, all their complicated undertakings *are* probably necessary to induce forced learning. They are also necessary in order to make schoolpeople themselves feel important. But none of it should intimidate you. Most of what teachers actually know about teaching has to do with classroom management (aka 'discipline'). In other words, most of what they know is stuff that obviously wouldn't matter if you were learning what you wanted to learn.

But schools push you beyond intimidation; they *shame* you into believing you need them. By giving out grades, they cancel people's faith in their perfectly good brains. Once you accept a report card's verdict that you're not so bright, you're hardly in a position to say you don't need school. If they happen to decide you *are* intelligent, you have the opposite problem – your ego is addicted. You 'succeed' in school, so why risk leaving it for a world where you might not get straight As?

It boils down to something called 'blaming the victim': school blames you instead of itself for your intellectual influenza. After first grade, you forget about your growing supply of natural curiosity. When they tell you the reason you don't do your schoolwork well enough is that you have no drive, curiosity or love of learning, you start believing them. By the time they tell you that if you can't make it *with* school, you certainly can't make it *without* school, you're really lost.

Obviously, schools need you to believe that you couldn't learn without them. Once they convince you of this, through intimidation and shame, it's over; you submit without much argument to 12 years of it. You become susceptible to the illogical kind of line one of my colleagues fed his students when they didn't finish their work: 'OK, don't turn in your homework. Grow up and be a junkie.'

The good part is that once you recognize their game for what it is, you can think about it clearly and start trusting yourself again.

So, dear reader, here we are at the end of another chapter. I invite you to sit down with your feet up and reflect upon your values and goals. Do they mesh with school? Are you tickled pink to have your mind programed into Obedient Worker mode? To cash in your cultural heritage for Mainstream Suburbia-think? To be babysat 35 hours every week?

Yes? Good girl. Good boy. Just put your feet back down, sit a little straighter, please, and do not look to the left or right.

No? Uh-oh. Welcome. Read on

4 | Schoolteachers: The People versus the Profession

This book has no intention of lessening your appreciation for the people who teach. Yet, my commentary in this chapter is both sweet and sour. On the one hand, I want to acknowledge the wonderful qualities teachers have, and to explain a few difficult and ironic aspects of their profession. In general, it is not the teachers' fault that school is bad – although if they all left there would be no more school. On the other hand, I want to point out some less healthy aspects of common teacher personalities, to help you understand some of the guilt-dynamics you may feel at school, and to help you give yourself permission to leave.

Most teachers are generous, intelligent, beautiful people. Some are very talented or knowledgeable in their fields and would make great mentors or tutors outside the constraints of school. Many have given up chances to make lots of money because they believe in teaching even though it pays poorly. Especially if they are men, they sometimes endure years of being hassled by their families – 'Why don't you find a *real* career?' In any grip-on-reality contest, your average schoolteacher would win four times as many trophies as your average company executive.

Most teachers and other people in schools believe they are doing the right thing. They are not preventing democracy, freedom and education on purpose. When they do purposely prevent freedom, they think it is in your best interest, so that you'll be ready to work hard and 'succeed' in your afterlife. Respect their good intentions.

A few teachers are amazing enough to conquer. In their classes, something strong and beautiful happens, despite all the unpleasant forces of the opposition. Also, just because someone teaches doesn't mean they're mentally 'in league' with the school system. Many teachers start teaching in the first place because they think school is a bad place and they hope to make it better. Unfortunately, most of these teachers either end up quitting or else compromising their ideals – the system is so much bigger and stronger than they are. Still, a lot of teachers have a few years of passionate vision in them. Don't assume, because schools squash you, that teachers *want* to squash you. For most teachers, as well as students, the world will be a more chocolate place when school is not compulsory and full of administrative backwash.

Which brings me to a different point. Not all teachers want to run your lives, but they have no choice. They *must* 'manage' you. It is their job to give you Fs if you don't do 'your' work, to report your absences, to make you be quiet, to assign homework, to enforce school rules they don't personally believe in, such as 'You have to wear socks with tennis shoes', and 'no leaning back in your chair'. No teacher could keep a job if she said, 'It doesn't matter whether you do the homework tonight. If you'd prefer to spend more time doing something else, please do. You won't get a zero, and I won't be disappointed in you.' Teachers' job descriptions leave no way for them to treat you with the respect they would show their friends.

I can illustrate my point in a backwards way by telling you about a day I just couldn't do the job. I was substitute teaching physics. One of the people in the class, a 14-year-old boy, was a good friend of mine. Because he was there, I came in the door as myself, not Miss Llewellyn. The class zoomed out of control. Airplanes flew into the blackboard; everyone talked while I gave the assignment; two boys in dark glasses put their feet on their desks, leaned back, crossed their arms, and grinned. Any other day, I would have snapped into the role they'd created for me. I was good at it. 'Ladies and *gent*lemen,' ran my usual substitute talk, '*where* is your self-respect? Mr Washington and Mr Garcia, please remove the glasses. If any of you would care to visit the office, you can let me know by sending another airplane in this direction. Any questions?'

But with Otto's perceptive eyes on me, I couldn't bring myself to say the words. In his presence, they seemed suddenly so petty and artificial. They had nothing to do with Grace Llewellyn. I did a lousy job that day because Otto brought a flash of a deeper reality. What that says about the days I *could* do my job is unpleasant indeed.

Something that surprised me when I started teaching was that my fellow teachers were terrific people. Almost all of them. That hurt my brain a little. I remembered having a lot of mean, stupid teachers in school – was I wrong? Or had the teaching profession changed radically in five years?

The truth didn't strike until I substitute taught for a few months in my own former junior high and high schools, rubbing my adult shoulders with the very same people who used to grade my tests and ask me not to read novels during their brilliant lectures. All of them were terrific people – in my adult company. From the glimpses I caught of them in their classes, and the student conversations I overheard in the halls, some were apparently still mean and stupid in their classrooms.

I started wondering how many teenagers thought *I* was mean and stupid when I stood in front of a classroom. And over the next few years, I came to believe firmly: the majority of teachers are amazing, intelligent, generous and talented people. But the role they are forced to play in school keeps them from showing you these sides of themselves. Their talent and energy is drained instead by their constant task of telling people what to do.

Not everything about teachers is terrific, of course. Like a lot of other kinds of people, they have their weak points as well as their good qualities. And some of the things for which we praise teachers most loudly are the ways they cause the most harm.

For instance, many teachers seem to have an inborn desire to run other people's lives (to 'help people'). Even if it were tolerable that others should run our lives, teachers are rarely any good at doing so, being as fully human as their students.

It makes sense that people who like controlling others gravitate toward teaching. It's a great profession for people who wish they were a king or God. Me, for example. When I was six or so I used to love to play school. I was the teacher. I called it Pee-Wee. My brothers, the students, were usually unenthusiastic but I was older and I could bribe or force them into it. I choreographed dances and made them learn, pinching them when they lost the beat. In general, I didn't feel my own life was enough territory – I wanted to design theirs too (just like my teachers got to design *my* life, I might add). It is this controlling and designing quality that disturbs me again and again in teachers – including myself – and in administrators. The most dangerous people in life are often those who want most to help you, whether or not you want their 'help'. 'She's the sort of woman who lives for others,' wrote C S Lewis. 'You can tell the others by their hunted expression.'

Teaching also turns you into an automatic authority figure. It is ideal work for anyone who likes to feel superior. No one questions much where your authority comes from, or how much it is deserved.

Moreover, being a teacher is a perfect way to get attention and praise for being selfless and generous. Do you know anyone who loves to suffer nobly, as long as someone's watching and feeling sorry for them? A lot of teachers do. They thrive not on money, but on the brownie points they get for staying up all night to mark tests, for earning abominable salaries, for driving across town in a blizzard to rent *The Story of English* on video, for explaining fractions 30 times to Suki on Friday afternoon, for neglecting their own favorite sports in order to coach basketball. Unfortunately, people who are good at suffering and working hard in public are also good at giving other people guilt trips.

What do we need instead of people who love to sacrifice themselves for others? We need people who do what they most love, and do it well, and let others hang around or join in unforced, and share their knowledge instead of hoarding it. This behavior requires true generosity, because it allows other people to be equals, not helpless victims.

Another unfortunate aspect of teacher personalities is a limited perspective. Most have not worked at other kinds of jobs, beyond summers at a cash register. Like you, they have spent all their lives at school. This leaves them almost incapable of imagining their students' potential futures. They can't help but communicate to you their narrow sense of the possibilities in life.

Finally, there is nothing wrong with teaching, only with teaching in the conditions of compulsory school. Lots of people do learn certain things best by being taught or shown. So don't limit yourself by assuming that teachers in school are the same as teachers out of school. Teachers out of school – in a martial arts studio, a book discussion group or a community education French class – can be themselves and teach from their hearts. Also, since you are not *required* to undergo the teaching, you will stay only if their methods work for you. When choice, freedom and individuality are introduced into teaching, it can be wonderful for everyone involved.

5 | The Power and Magic of Adolescence versus the Insufferable Tedium of School

> Youth is the time to go flashing from one end of the world to the other both in mind and body; to try the manners of different nations; to hear the chimes at midnight; to see sunrise in town and country; to be converted at a revival; to circumnavigate the metaphysics, write halting verses, run a mile to see a fire, and wait all day long in the theatre to applaud 'Hernani'.
>
> Robert Louis Stevenson, *Crabbed Age and Youth*

If you've ever read any anthropology, you've noticed that primal cultures simmer up all of their mystery and magic and power and ask their teenagers to drink deeply.

A 16-year-old Dakota boy fasts until an empowering vision overtakes him. A newly menstruating Apache girl becomes the goddess White Painted Woman in an intense, joyful, theatrical ritual which lasts four days. All over the planet, traditional cultures provide various ritual experiences to adolescents, bringing them into contact with the deepest parts of themselves and their heritage.

There is danger and pain, as well as beauty and exultation, in some of these traditional ways of initiating people into adulthood. I don't want to make any shallow statement that we've got it all wrong because we don't ask pubescent boys to endure three days of biting wasps.

But I would like you to reflect for a minute on the contrast between the way our society initiates its young and the vivid undertakings of the primal world.

What do you get instead of vision? You get school – and

all the blind passivity and grey monotone it trains into you.

For an institution to ask you, during some of your most magical years, to sit still and be good and read quietly for six or more hours each day is barely thinkable, let alone tolerable. How do you feel when the sun comes out in March and makes the most golden day imaginable, but you have to stay in and clean your room?

In case you've lost touch with your burgeoning beauty, let me remind you that that's exactly what's going on, for at least six years of your teenaged schooling. Adolescence is a time of dreaming, adventure, risk, sweet wildness and intensity. It's the time for you to 'find yourself', or at least go looking. The sun is rising on your life. Your body is breaking out of its cocoon and ready to try wings. But you have to stay in – for *such* a long time – and keep your pencils sharpened. School is bad for your spirit.

It's no accident, I'm sure. The way our society is set up now, something's got to prevent visionary experience. Otherwise, 90 per cent of our monoculture would shatter. People who are fully and permanently awakened to the wildness and beauty in and around them make lousy wage-slaves. On the other hand, people who are *not* distracted by a wellspring of spiritual and sexual yearnings can assemble clock radios or automobiles very quickly, or focus their intellects on monthly sales charts.

More importantly, unawakened people are less likely to question the things in our society which are horrifically dull and ridiculous. The point of seeking any kind of visionary experience is to *see*. When vision comes to you, eternity is its black velvet backdrop. Everything else comes out on the stage to sing and dance. Some of it fits in with the grandeur of that backdrop, and some of it only clashes, looking ugly and cheap. You end up wanting to adjust your life so that it's full of stuff that fits in with eternity, and not crammed with things that don't matter.

Therefore, one reason many primal cultures can

confidently guide their young toward visionary experiences is that they're not worried. They don't have to worry that the visions will show anything horrible about the society itself. If there *is* something going wrong with the cultural state of affairs, they want to know, so they can mend it.

In the industrialized world the opposite is true. When you have a messy house, you don't offer a magnifying glass to your guests. You probably don't even open the curtains and let the light in.

If we encouraged teenagers to seek visions, democracy would get a boost, but the powers of mass production and rat racing consumerism would take a dive. We would see that far too much of what we accept as 'reality' is a blasphemy against true reality. Since our consumptive culture is out of balance with the rest of the universe, it would look very bad under the inspection of visionary young people. Get it? Western civilization does not invite its young to seek visions, because those visions would force a big change.

No force of dullness and ignorance is strong enough, however, to stop you from seeking. Eternity, God, Goddess – whatever you call it – is too strong. It will get in, though it has to battle school and other strongholds of society. Writers and artists bring us some inklings, though when school introduces us to them, it nearly destroys their potency.

The Big Mystery creeps in through all your fascinations – music with heavy pulses and strange lyrics, sexual fantasies and experiences, the occult, drugs (including alcohol). Obviously, some of these things can be taken to unhealthy excess.

Unfortunately, most adults refuse to acknowledge the powerful impulse behind any of these activities, labeling them as 'bad', as if that would make them go away. Why? Their own visionary tendencies got canceled out by society at sweet 16. Misery, as they say, loves company. It is incredibly painful for an emotional cripple to be around someone who is emotionally free. And so most adults would rather pretend desperately to visionary teenagers that the world is nothing more than green lawns, white socks and recently sanitized carpets.

Visionary tendencies come in dark and light, or a combination thereof.

Some teenagers want dark experiences. They walk in cemeteries at night. They write stories about suicide; they are obsessed with black clothing and Pink Floyd lyrics. None of it means they are 'bad' or twisted. When they are finished playing with the dark, they will understand the light much better. If they are ignored or ridiculed, maybe they will do something drastic, but their search is usually only an earnest attempt to understand the depths.

Others gravitate toward the light – daytime psychedelic colors, long solitary walks. They determine to become a dancer or artist instead of something 'realistic'. If their family is sedately Catholic, maybe they go to the Assembly of God and speak in tongues. If their family goes to the Assembly of God, maybe they climb a hill and offer flowers to Apollo.

Schools – and many parents – lie a lot at this point, telling you you're out of touch with reality. The truth is, you're out of touch with the expectations and patterns of an *un*real, man-made industrial society. You are *in* touch with the reality that counts. Look at the Milky Way some night and think about it. You'll know.

Furthermore ...

Schools – and this society they represent – go beyond blocking your visionary tendencies. They further cripple you by making fun of you, as if you were not quite human, the new niggers. Why? Probably because every hierarchical society seems to need people to put down, and women and people of African descent won't take it any more.

Another reason adults make fun of you is that they're jealous. Teenagers are beautiful and fresh; the perfume of a flower is concentrated in the bud. Yes, many teenagers are awkward, pimpled, or strangely tall and thin. Far more adults, however, are awkward (having forgotten how to use their bodies), sallow-skinned (too much sitting in air-conditioned offices) and heavy (not enough skateboarding).

A healthy adult society would acknowledge the beauty of youth, make up some good poems about it, and then not think about it too much. There are certainly more productive activities in life than fixating on the rosy cheeks you'll never have again. But since we do not have a healthy adult society, we get all bent out of shape over it, create a cult of young-beautiful-people-in-magazines, and punish real live teenagers by telling them they are ugly.

Just in case you do understand that you are beautiful, they make sure that you can't appreciate it by telling you that you are confused and overly emotional during these traumatic years – and for Pete's sake don't go and make any decisions for yourself, and don't let loose and have any free wild experiences with life. Dogs in mangers, we turn the power of adolescence into a weak disease. Teachers sit in the teachers' lounge and laugh about you behind your backs.

Isn't he cute, they say. Poor Kristy, with no idea of how she sticks out in that magenta skirt. This, from people who are overweight, in ruts, out of touch with their dreams, insecure and otherwise at least as imperfect as the subjects of their conversation. Thank God I'm not that age any more, says Mrs Wallace, leaning her double chin over her desk. We read tacky cute articles in *Family Circle* called 'How to Survive the Terrible Teens: An Owner's Guide'. The owner being the parent, of course. *School*, yes, is something to survive, but being a teenager is something that flies.

We force you to act younger than you are, legally withholding your ability to control your own life. In the

World Book encyclopedia it says, 'Most teenagers mature psychologically at the rate set by their society. As a result, psychological adolescence normally lasts at least as long as the period of legal dependence.' Certainly, there is no *biological* limitation to teenage independence. In other times and places, teenagers have commonly married, raised children, held jobs, operated businesses and, occasionally, ruled countries.

'It seems you're talking about more than just schools here. Aren't you getting off the point a bit?'

Yes, school is not the only villain in the war against whole adolescence. But it *is* our culture's deathly substitute for powerful growing experiences. It *is* the way we take your time so you don't explore your own inklings of truth. It *is* the place where you learn to be passive instead of active. Quitting school isn't going to guarantee you a healthy, passionate adolescence, but at least it will remove the biggest obstacle against that flowering.

6 | And a Few Other Miscellaneous Abominations

Aside from the previously described big reasons to quit school, there are dozens of random miscellaneous ones, which are also important.

School puts you into intense, forced contact with people your own age. It discourages you from making friends with other people. If you don't like being shut up with your peers all day, that doesn't mean you're socially maladjusted. Why should you prefer the company of hundreds of people your own age to a more healthy mix of people? Adults have been around longer than teenagers. Therefore, they have experiences and perspectives that teenagers lack.

When adults aren't your schoolteachers (and therefore have no control over you), most will treat you like real people. Outside school, if you're busy doing something, most adults won't think of you as a 'kid' – at least not for long. You will learn from them, and they will learn from you. Also, you can have friends younger than yourself.

School teaches frenzy. When adults get turned loose after college, lots of them go to bookstores and buy self-help books. These books help them unlearn the lessons of school. Slow down, they say. Concentrate only on the important things. Don't make yourself feel guilty for not 'doing everything'. Live your life the way *you* want to live it. If you quit school now, maybe you can reclaim this childhood wisdom before you sprout wrinkles, and save 30 dollars or so in self-help books.

If you go to school, you almost have to be a jerk to other people, to yourself, or to both. When other people are jerks, life loses a bit of its sheen. When *you* are a jerk, life loses a lot of its sheen. Yet school sometimes gives you no choice.

A simple example is my day in May at the natural history museum, a school field trip. The students were told to sit quietly and listen to the tour guide. The tour guide stood in front of the exhibits, blocking them. She rambled dully, as tour guides are prone to do. The exhibits, on the other hand, were stunning and infinitely more 'educational' than any dry-rot lecture or textbook.

The students had two choices. They could show the expected 'respect' to the tour guide and sit quietly, bored as bureaucrats, disrespecting themselves. Or they could show 'disrespect' and disobedience to the guide and stand up, walk around, and look and learn. Andy did. Andy got scolded. I hate remembering.

Schools create meaningless, burdensome problems for you to solve. School claims to be a system which is accountable to the larger world around it. In other words, what you learn in school is supposed to help you make sense of the rest of the world. In good moments, you do learn useful information. But much of your time in school is spent simply learning how to get along in *school*. Schoolpeople impose elaborate homework policies, consequences and language – 'You're earning an F. That's a problem. How are you going to solve it?' They call things like grades and homework your 'responsibility', without giving you the slightest choice in accepting that responsibility.

Schoolpeople justify their actions by saying they're teaching you to be responsible and 'follow through' later in school and later in life. But all this is so different from real life that it's ridiculous. In real life, you *choose* what to take responsibility for.

Schools give you an incurable guilt trip. At the school I taught in, we watched a videotape as part of a study skills unit. It was about getting good grades. You *should* get good grades, the speaker kept saying. If you are capable of an A, he said, but you only get a C, that ought to be unacceptable to you. Maybe, he added, not quite joking, you ought to make yourself sleep on the floor that night.

In a parent–teacher conference, a wealthy, 'successful' father complained about Jill's (fake name) Cs and Bs. 'I wouldn't care if she couldn't do the work,' he said, 'I'm just angry that she doesn't. Why does she throw her talent away?' As if getting Cs and Bs meant that one was doing nothing with one's life. It all boils down to a guilt trip if you spend your energy on what you care about, and pats on the head if you forget who you are and do what you're told.

Schools blame victims. In other words, they inflict all manner of nasty experiences and expectations on you, and then tell you it's your fault for not liking it. They blame *you* for *their* problems. An advice column in the magazine *Scholastic Choices*, March 1990, ran this letter:

> I'm 13 and I want to quit school. I think it's boring. Besides my teachers are all mean [unkind]. I think I could get a job on a farm and make a living that way. What should I do?

Easy enough to answer – 'Quit school, of course. It *is* boring. Teachers *are* unkind, though it's part of their job to be that way. Work on a farm if you *want*, but as a 13-year-old you shouldn't have to worry about earning a living.' The king of the advice column, however, had different ideas:

> The way you write and express yourself tells me that you are smart, though unhappy, and are blaming your dissatisfaction on things outside of yourself. [In other words, you should be blaming your dissatisfaction on yourself.] You don't feel bored because school is boring or teachers are mean. You don't feel secure or comfortable with yourself. If you can't settle these feelings in a year or so, counselors can help you learn to understand your feelings more clearly.

No comment.

There's more to life. You yearn. You know that life is *not* the color of linoleum halls or the drab hum of industrial lighting or the slow ticking of the clock. Look at the stars. Look hard at the faces of people throwing frisbees in a park, singing in church, passing the potatoes, planting tomatoes, mending a kitchen table or the engine in an old truck. Look at a baby or a piece of handcarved furniture or a 300-year-old tree or a pebble or a worm or the sweater your grandmother knitted for you. Perhaps school's greatest danger is that it may convince you life is nothing more than an institutionalized rat race.

School, of course, is not the only big gray institution our country relies on to suck the spirit out of its people. Hospitals, big office buildings and numerous governmental interferences pull the same trick. But school is the first such institution most of us endure, and it wears down our resistance to the later ones. It makes them seem normal; it makes us feel greedy or idealistic or stupidly poetic when we hear our hearts telling us, 'It shouldn't be like this! I'm better than this! I was made for more wonderful things.'

School conditions you to live for the future, rather than to live in the present. In GWS no. 39, Marti Holmes, mother of a 15-year-old, wrote, 'Homeschooling has not closed any doors that I can see, and has provided rich, full years of living (rather than "preparing for life").' Contrary to the teachings of school, you are not in dress rehearsal. More than anything else, this book is about living – now, as well as 20 years from now. Quit school before it convinces you life is nothing but a waiting game, an *ugly* waiting game. 'We are always getting ready to live, but never living,' wrote Emerson. Don't let the schoolpeople write that on your tombstone.

7 | But Miss Llewellyn ...

Panic strikes your hungry heart. You cry out: 'I want to be free ... But I also want to go to college and get a good job! My friends are all in school, and what would I do without football?'

Yeah, there are a lot of buts. They all have answers. Let's look. One at a time.

'But I want to go to college and get a good job!' Fine. Neither depend on graduating from school. For college, see chapter 25. As far as jobs go, yes, there is plenty of prejudice against 'drop-outs', and if you refer to yourself as one, forget it. If, on the other hand, you call yourself a homeschooler or explain exactly what you did instead of school, and why, intelligent employers will smile approvingly.

However ... be prepared to change your thoughts about what you want out of life. School shapes so much of your mind that when you leave it, you may no longer feel certain that you want college – or you may feel *more* certain. You may grow different ideas as to what kind of work you want to do, and your definition of a 'good job' may change. Furthermore, by quitting school and beginning to make independent choices, you run the risk of turning into a person who sculpts creative, fulfilling ways to earn money without reporting to a boss.

Does school actually prepare you for the world of work? If you plan to have sweep floors or assemble plastic toys all your life, then yes, school will break your spirit ahead of time so you don't fight when you get nothing wonderful out of adulthood. In fact school will condition you to accept *any* kind of work you don't love, whether as an MD or a secretary.

School, however, does not prepare you to identify your own dreams and make them come true.

'But I have to learn school subjects – science, history, literature, etc – because they will make me into a Proper Citizen!' Yes, investigating all these subjects will probably make you a better citizen.

Going to school all day and obeying authority as if you lived in a dictatorship will make you a worse one.

What's a patriot to do? Quit school and learn all that juicy stuff and do your best to prevent bad stories (histories) from repeating themselves. Read widely and thoughtfully. The more you do, the less all of us will need to worry about our future. Education, as they call it, should make you a more intelligent voter, and more importantly a good leader in any situation – serving on a city planning committee, nudging your aunt Marcia to recycle her beer cans. Certainly, the more informed and thoughtful citizens are, the wiser decisions they ought to make as a group.

True, people who don't go to school might end up knowing different types of things from schoolteenagers, depending on their interests. This, too, is a sign of good citizenship. A community is made more intelligent if its people bring many different perspectives and a wide expanse of knowledge. If you wind up knowing more about Jean-Jacques Rousseau than Martin Luther King, or Hopi farming practices instead of the structure of DNA, or motorcycle engines instead of computers, your citizenship will be as intact as the Jones's. *More* intact, actually, because you'll like what you know, and you'll keep it in mind whenever you think about anything.

Furthermore, any sort of learning is your responsibility. Your life and time belong to you and the universe, and to the government only to the extent that it is in harmony with the universe. Anyway, lots of 'well-educated' people are rotten citizens. So read to feed your hungry head, not to fulfill some pinched sense of duty.

'*But my school has a good choir!*' '*I live to play football!*' '*And what about me? I want to be Miss Drill Team USA!*' Some schools do offer outstanding performing and sports opportunities that are difficult to find elsewhere. My own melodious memory of singing with and playing piano for two outstanding choirs in high school almost compensates for the lackluster hours I spent enduring everything else. Almost, but not quite. If you truly love your opportunity to belong to a school team or performing group, consider two things.

First, you *can* leave school and continue to participate in these activities – either at school itself or elsewhere. Second, if you can't replace the activity, or participate in it without being enrolled in school full time, is it terrific enough that it makes up for the drudgery of the rest of school? If you want to play professional football, maybe so. Everyone makes trade-offs; millions of adults live somewhere without liking it because it offers them work they do like. But if you'd have as much fun playing hockey with an independent league as playing school football, get clear. Cash in your shoulder pads for freedom.

'*But what if all I want to do instead of school is watch TV all day?*' Well. Don't misunderstand me. I would turn heartsick and give up if this book led to a cult of TV parasites who soaped instead of schooled, and I personally would rather be stuck going to school all day than force-fed Channel Zero for six hours.

However, I don't worry. If you think what you want most is to soak in sit-coms all day, probably all you really need and want is a vacation. After a week or so of TV, you'll feel restless and ready to move on. If you don't yet have any ideas, you'll be ready to find some. Furthermore, I'm convinced that addiction to TV is a by-product of schooling. School doesn't encourage you to take action. Once you get used to sitting passively all day, it's hard to be a person with initiative. But school doesn't really kill your brain; it only sends it into deep freeze. After it thaws, you'll want more than TV.

'But what if I don't get along with my parents and don't want them to be my teachers?' or *'What if my parents both work and can't stay at home to homeschool me?'* If unschooling or homeschooling depended on parents to be teachers, I'd never write a book about it. Lots of teenagers get along with their parents (especially teenagers who don't go to school) but lots don't. And no matter how well you get along with your parents, that doesn't mean you'd like them to direct your education. I would have *hated* for my parents to be my 'teachers' in the school sense. The conflicts and power struggles we already had could only have intensified.

On the other hand, I would have loved to have been an 'unschooler', in charge of my own education. If my parents and I had known about unschooling and tried it, I think they would have been wise and trusting enough to let me explore independently. It is likely that our relationship would have improved since I would have felt better about my own life. But I would have fiercely resisted any well-meant parental attempts to control my learning.

So, once and for all, let's get this straight: I am not talking about turning your parents into your main teachers, unless that is specifically what you and they want to do. Your teachers can be: yourself, books, basketball courts, adults you talk to or write letters to, your friends, museums, plants and rivers.

I know of many unschoolers, by the way, whose parents both work away from home. Not only that, but in *GWS* there are occasional letters from parents with *younger* children who stay at home without adults during the days – and like it, and don't die. More importantly, the majority of teenaged homeschoolers who wrote to me said that their parents played a minor role in their education. They answer questions when asked, talk a lot, and sometimes share their expertise *when the teenager is interested.* In other families, the parents really do get involved, learning alongside their children, but that happens more often at younger ages. Both the parents and teenagers who contacted me seemed to share an understanding that teenagers are old enough to direct their own education and activities.

To be sure, there are families where the parent takes over the role of teacher and principal – sometimes in a very authoritarian way. The idea repels me, but if you like it that's your business.

'But I'm lazy! If no one makes me learn, I won't.' How do you know you're lazy when you've never had the chance to choose what to work at? If you call yourself lazy, your biggest job in unschooling will be remembering, glimmer by glimmer, how much you loved to learn before school took that love away. Frogs, wheels, words, blocks, dogs – when you were a little kid, the world fascinated and dazzled you. Also, you will need to allow yourself to admire ('learn') the things that still sparkle in your kaleidoscope, whatever they are.

And laziness shouldn't be confused with Zen-like tranquillity. 'Lazy' travelers who hang out in a little Peruvian village for a week will soak up the life and ambiance of Peru far more than the typical tourist who in one week sucks in Macchu Picchu, three market towns, four museums, two ancient ruins and one horse ride along the Urubamba River. People who find ways to get out of the 'rat race' or the obscene commercialism attending Christmas improve the quality of their lives by deliberately avoiding frantic, mindless activity. The same goes for learning: watching the sky for two hours will do more for anyone's cortex than a harried afternoon of longitude worksheets.

'But my friends are at school!' Ah yes. The big one. So get your friends to quit with you. See your schoolfriends on evenings or weekends when they're finished with

homework. Make new friends through your interests.

Anyway, stop and think about it. We are social creatures, yes – but not *institutional* creatures.

How much communication do you usually have with your friends at school? Except at lunch and breaks, you are rarely supposed to talk with them. If you have friends in some of your classes, you see them – but I'm not sure this is the way to build trust, compassion, generosity and other qualities integral to healthy friendship. In some courses you compete for As with the other students. Your discussion is overseen and censored by a teacher. Working together is called cheating. What really gets cheated is your ability to help each other climb.

And remember: your enemies are in school too. Adults control and humiliate teenagers, and teenagers even things out for themselves by controlling and humiliating each other. Few people emerge from school's obsessive popularity and conformity contests without scars.

'*But there's nothing better to do!*' One of my favorite and usually most profound students gave this sloppy slogan as the reason he'd stay in school even if he didn't have to. He explained a bit by saying that he was too young to have a job and anyway all his friends were there, so he could neither work nor socialize. Indeed, without a meaningful alternative and good company, school might seem the least of several evils.

Yes, this society is hostile and unwelcoming to teenagers, and laws do prevent teenagers from working for money in certain situations. However, with a small carton of creativity and confidence, you'll dream up an infinite number of enjoyable and enlightening alternatives. That's what Parts 2, 3 and 4 of this book are for.

'*But it's easy to go to school – I don't have to think for myself!*' To you, I have nothing to say. Stay right there at your graffiti-adorned desk. When you turn 18, proceed directly into the army. Be all that you can be, according to somebody else.

'Miss Llewellyn, you're not being nice.'

Sorry. You're right. By the way, you can call me Grace.

Who would consciously stay at school just to avoid thinking for themselves? No one, probably. And if everything we did was based on conscious, rational choice, life would be simple indeed.

But we are not such rational creatures. Until we face them, fears from our subconscious can ruin our lives. If you don't tingle at the thought of quitting school, please look inside. Think hard about whether you're afraid of independence. It's natural to be scared of facing the drums in your own dancing shoes; if you think for yourself, you have no one but yourself to blame for your successes and failures.

Adults, too, hide from the chance to direct their own lives and minds – which is why a lot of them stay in 'safe' jobs they detest all their lives, idly fantasizing about the career risk they will take when the kids are grown, or the adventures they will seek once they retire.

Yes, when we live in dreams, we can imagine our 'futures' in tissue-wrapped perfection. When we get out of dreams into the present, we find no such perfection. Instead, we find life. It's scary stuff. But it's *real*. Acknowledge your fear, but don't give into it. Dance bravely and brightly. Learn to be a human bean and not instant mashed potatoes.

8 | Your Allies among the Rich and Famous

I suppose it shouldn't have surprised me, but it did. I'd heard of a few 'famous' people who hadn't gone to school, so I went to the library to check up on them. From the reference section I took down a stack of *Current Biography Yearbooks*. I started by looking up the names on my list, but pretty soon I was just turning pages and laughing. Why?

1 On average, one out of every five or six people featured had dropped out of school or else not attended much formal school. (The *Current Biography Yearbook*[6] is published every year. It contains hundreds of short biographies on people who are currently prominent in some field – worldwide government leaders, entertainers, scientists, writers, artists.)

2 In almost all the biographies, it was clear that the forces which had shaped these brilliant lives had little or nothing to do with school. Instead, other experiences had inspired and nurtured them.

   For instance, Luc Montagnier, French virologist famous for his research on the Aids virus, was inspired to become a scientist mainly because his father kept a laboratory in the garage, because he was allowed to have his own laboratory in the basement, and because at the age of 15, he watched his grandfather die of cancer.[7]

   Also, for instance, Steven Spielberg learned film-making by experimenting with his father's 8mm camera. At school, he spent a lot of time making films in order to escape studying algebra and French. Later, he sneaked on to film sets to watch (his high school grades were too low to get him into film school).[8]

3 Lots of famous people had to go to school – they'd probably never heard of 'unschooling' – but made nasty comments about it.

I am not bringing up the subject of rich famous people to suggest that it is necessarily fulfilling to be rich and famous. However, information like this is a good kick in the pants for all the unimaginative, illogical people who believe quitting school generates 'failure'.

Keep your ears open, and compile your own list of admirable independent learners. Here is part of mine, from various sources including encyclopedias and *Current Biography*.

Some people who dropped out of high school or otherwise escaped much or all of the usual teenage schooling: Ansel Adams, Joan of Arc, Roseanne Barr, Irving Berlin, Rosamond Bernier, Claude Berri, William Blake, Art Blakey, John Boorman, Pearl Buck, Liz Claiborne, Samuel Clemens (Mark Twain), Buffalo Bill Cody, Noel Coward, Charles Dickens, Bo Diddley, Thomas Edison, Benjamin Franklin, Henry Ford, George Gershwin, Whoopi Goldberg, Samuel Gompers, Maxim Gorki, Robin Graham, Patrick Henry, Eric Hoffer, John Houston, John Paul Jones, Cyndi Lauper, William Lear, Abraham Lincoln, Jack London, Beryl Markham, Liza Minnelli, Wolfgang Amadeus Mozart, Sean O'Casey, Florence Nightingale, Beatrix Potter, David Puttnam, Keith Richards, Clement W Stone, Randy Travis, Frank Lloyd Wright, Orville and Wilbur Wright, Brigham Young.[9]

Also: one-third of the men who signed the Declaration of Independence, the Articles of Confederation, and the Constitution of the United States had no more than a few months of schooling up their sleeves. Historian Harry G

Good describes several of them:

> Stephen Hopkins of Rhode Island, a farm boy, became a practical surveyor and learned politics as moderator of town meetings. Roger Sherman of Connecticut was apprenticed to a shoemaker and became successively a writer, publisher, and lawyer ... Others read medical books and helped a doctor in his practice.[10]

For more, browse through any year's edition of *Current Biography*.

WANNA-BE UNSCHOOLERS

Brilliant people often got that way not because of school, but despite it. For instance, Woody Allen said, 'I loathed every day and regret every day I spent in school. I like to be taught to read and write and add and then be left alone.'[11] Winston Churchill said, 'I was happy as a child with my toys in my nursery. I have been happier every year since I became a man. But this interlude of school makes a sombre grey patch upon the chart of my journey. It was an unending spell of worries that did not then seem petty, and of toil uncheered by fruition; a time of discomfort, restriction and purposeless monotony.'[12] Pulitzer-prize winning historian Edmund Morris hated high school, and 'entertained himself by writing novels "behind cover of an atlas at the rearmost possible desk of every class".' And Charles Trenet, French singer, songwriter and writer, went to a Catholic school – the 'Free School of the Trinity', about which he said, 'The school might have been free, but I was shut up inside.'[13]

PART 2 | The First Steps

9 | The Perhaps Delicate Parental Issue

Most unschooled people have, in the past, been out of school because of their *parents'* beliefs. This is where the book in your hands tries to dream something new – that *you*, because of *your* initiative and *your* yearning, march in front of your own parade.

'Lovely,' you say, 'but what that means is that I have to convince my parents that unschooling is a good thing for me and them.'

Yes.

Fortunately, with a little care and planning, you will probably be able to help them see the light. Ideally, it will go well enough for your parents to support and encourage you without entangling themselves too much in your hair, and to become so inspired by you that their own lives become richer and braver.

First, though, let's confront some fears *you* might have about unschooling and parents.

YOUR FEARS

'What if I don't get along with my parents? Won't unschooling just make it worse?' I have some comfort to offer you. Unschooling, generally, seems to make parents into allies and friends rather than disciplinarians and authority figures. At least, dozens of unschooling parents and teenagers have told me so. Joel Maurer, 13, says, 'My mom

likes me better than when I was in school.' Judy Garvey wrote in *GWS* no. 70, 'Homeschooling is so much easier than having to deal with children who have been in school all day.' Another parent wrote in *GWS* no. 26:

> Have other parents noticed a very easy adolescence with unschooled kids? I think that my 15-year-old son's early acquaintance with responsibility for his own actions has made it unnecessary for him to rebel and fight for independence. He is willing to accept my judgment at times because it is offered as one adult to another and not as a restriction on a kid who doesn't know anything.

And a Canadian father wrote to me that homeschooling 'has greatly improved family dynamics since we have fewer time pressures and those we have are of our choosing. Both kids are really happy ... come to think of it my wife and I are not too glum ourselves!'

Many unschoolers told me that, once they left school, all kinds of family arguments and hostilities just disappeared. It makes sense; no more quarrels about grades or homework, no more need to take revenge on parents for what happens at school. If you still have doubts, think of activities you would enjoy away from home – volunteering, apprenticing, babysitting while you read or make notes.

'My parents have always hounded me about my schoolwork. I'm afraid if I quit school they'll be even worse, since they won't have any teachers to help "control" me.' Make sure when you discuss unschooling with them that they understand your need for independence. Make a point of talking with them often about your activities. Show them what you accomplish, or keep a daily log that they are welcome to read. If you admit your concerns as well as your joys, they will see that you are in touch with reality, and won't need to preach constantly. Ask their advice when you can – they will feel valued and it will encourage them to give up their controlling role in favor of a softer advisory one. *You* set the tone.

THE GENTLE ART OF PERSUASION

You know your parents. I don't. What causes giggling in one family might cause slamming doors in another. Perhaps your relationship with your parents is warm and trusting enough that you can simply bring your ideas up casually at the dinner table with confidence that they'll understand and support your decision to quit school. On the other hand, maybe you hide this book under your mattress and *know* they'll say no before you finish your first sentence. Most likely, you fit somewhere between these two extremes, and you should find at least some ideas in this chapter that enable you to convince your parents and then live happily with them for some more years.

Unless you know that your parents will agree easily, I suggest a bit of structure, planning and method. There are lots of ways you could organize this. You might start by asking them to attend a homeschoolers' meeting with you, or by leaving books on homeschooling lying around the house in conspicuous places.

You may want to write a proposal. Even if you're not sure exactly what you want to do once you're free, your parents can't help but be favorably impressed by a thoughtfully written plan of action. Also, writing the proposal will challenge you to think about some important questions, which will both prepare you to talk with your parents and also clear your vision as to what it is you hope to do with your new life. In the proposal, include the following:

- Your reasons for wanting to leave school.
- What you would like to do instead.
- Your academic plans.
- How you see your parents' roles in your new life and education.
- A statement that you will need a vacation at the beginning of your unschooling career to recover from

school. (If your parents are difficult to convince, you don't want to shock them by sleeping through the first two weeks of unschooling.)

- A tentative outline of the legal or official steps you will need to take together.
- A list of books you suggest they read.

Anticipate the questions and arguments your particular parents might come up with, and decide how you can most honestly and thoughtfully respond to them. Also, imagine all the secret fears they might have that could prevent them from supporting you. The more you understand about your parents' values and lives, the better. To get you started, here are some of the obvious questions some parents I know might bring up, along with ideas for possible responses.

'You've never done very well at school, even with all those teachers around to prod you along. How am I supposed to believe you could quit school and actually learn anything on your own?' If you've ever been interested in anything – in school or out – and gone after it in an independent way, remind them. If you've developed an interest but not developed it due to lack of time, point out that more time will help you to follow through. Explain that in order to learn, you must have the freedom to explore things that interest you. Ask them if *they* are any good at learning things on command. Ask them to think about the ways they learn – now, not in their ancient past.

Acknowledge that unschooling would require them to trust you to learn and grow independently, and that at first this might be very difficult for them. If you wish, tell them you could unschool on a trial basis. You might want to share other parents' experiences with them. A Brooklyn parent wrote in *GWS* no. 32:

> [My daughter] wouldn't let me tutor her and she wouldn't do all the educational things I had planned, like go to museums and stuff. She hung around in her bathrobe and drew pictures

all day. For nearly three years. Summers, too. Well, you should see her art work today. Fantastic!

Gwen A Meehan took her son Patrick out of school when he was 13, and wrote to me a year later:

> Pat had asked me after fourth grade (when he was about nine years old) to please, please let him stay at home and learn. My reaction was the same as most people's: (1) I didn't dream that it was, in fact, a legal option, (2) I couldn't imagine his not having daily, active social interaction with the other students, and (3), selfishly, 'There goes any time I might have for my own projects.' I'm not even mentioning the sheer terror at the idea of being his official *'teacher'*. Parenting is responsibility enough. (It turns out I was spooking myself all the way around! It has been a piece of cake!)
>
> I should have listened then. If I had, we could have avoided so much pain and so much lost self-esteem. I don't know if I'll ever see again the relaxed, happy, confident, healthy young person who went so happily into kindergarten ...'

'I'm not qualified to teach you' or 'I don't have time to teach you.' Point out that you're not asking them to be your teachers (unless you are), and that you can pursue your interests on your own and in the company of people with similar interests. Remind them that you know how to read, make friends, use the phone, write letters and look up books at the library. Ask them if they always need teachers when they become interested in a subject. If you currently ask them for help with homework, and expect to continue to ask for a similar amount of help, acknowledge this. Tell them that most unschooling parents do not *teach* their children, but rather allow them to learn on their own. Linda J Savelo, mother of 13-year-old Andrea, says, 'We're available whenever she needs us or is searching for answers. We suggest, support, make things available but trust her to search for herself what *she's* interested in.' Jade Crown, 14, whose mother is a single parent, says:

When people ask me if my parents teach me at home I tell them that my mom works full time and my dad lives on the other side of the country. My mom doesn't have extra time to tutor me in algebra because she works and cleans and cooks dinner every day (almost). One of the main reasons my mom was opposed to unschooling at first was because she was scared to leave me alone so much of the time. She often said, 'In a two-parent family, I might consider it. But it's not a choice for you right now.' I have proved her wrong. I have gained a lot of independence from unschooling alone, but I've also become better at finding the help I need. I have built a social structure outside of school (Good God! That too?) and found teachers and mentors to help me with the things I can't learn, or have no desire to learn by myself. I've also hooked up with other unschooling teenagers and built relationships with their parents. When I'm inspired to do something, I do it, and my mom is usually thrilled to hear about what I'm learning and who I meet. She once said to me that unschooling was the best decision she ever made as a parent. That made me feel really close to her. It's certainly one of the best decisions I ever made. She's become a big advocate (I never expected that) and we are both proud of each other.

In the Oregon Home Education Network Newsletter, longtime homeschooling parent Vivienne Edwards says, 'Many parents get worried that they will not be able to teach at the high school level. All you can do is help your children find environments where they can learn. This could be an apprenticeship, tutor, job, correspondence course, travel, neighbor, college, pen-pal, library, local business, volunteer job, museum, sport, vacation, ethnic neighborhood, church, family project – the list is endless, but all of these are valuable learning opportunities.'

Ruth McCutchen writes in *GWS* no. 52:

The most frequent response that I get nowadays to the statement that my children are homeschooled is, 'Really? How wonderful! I admire you, but I could *never* do that! I just don't have what it takes, etc, etc'. When I tell them that *I* don't do it, the *children* do and explain a bit what I mean, I'm met with incredulity ... Now that Deborah, Rebekah and Abigail are 17, 15 and 12, I find more and more that they really are doing it on their own. They long ago reached the point of asking me more questions that I *don't* know than ones that I *do*.

David and Micki Colfax, in *Homeschooling for Excellence*, write, 'In homeschooling, the children typically teach themselves, with the parents appropriately relegated to the job of suggesting courses of study and being available to answer questions – an uncomplicated process ...'

And in her book *And the Children Played*, Patricia Joudry writes, 'Some people think that if you're going to educate your children at home, you have to be constantly at the ready with blackboard and pointer. Not a bit: you have to do something much harder than that. Mind your own business.'

'I can believe you'll do fine in chemistry and history because you've always liked them, but what about learning Spanish?' You could either promise to do Spanish first every day, in order to relieve their anxiety, or you could try to help them understand that you don't need to learn Spanish now, and that, if and when you want it, you can learn it. You may decide to compromise at first, by structuring your study quite a bit, but chances are your parents will mellow in time. Ideally, they will be able to share the perspective of Rachel Diener, who writes about her 13-year-old son:

> His education is entirely self directed – that is, he chooses what he wants to learn and how and when he wants to learn it. As a result, if compared with his peers, he is far ahead in some areas (computer knowledge, electronics, vocabulary) and behind in some others (mathematical computation, handwriting skills). He and I are both satisfied with this. I think if he is allowed to focus on his strengths and pursue them to the limit rather than plodding along trying to remedy his weaknesses, he will be a happier and more successful person.

Far more important than the fears your parents will express are the fears they won't express. Your job is to guess what these fears might be, think them through, and then bring them up without directly accusing your parents of thinking this way. Here are some things your parents might feel but not be able to say.

'*I had to go to school and suffer. It would be too painful to see you go free when it's too late for me.*' Realize that if your parents agree with your feelings about school, that might force them to admit to themselves that a lot of their own schooling was a waste of time. Recognize that they are likely to feel a rush of despair and sense of loss over this, and that they may avoid these feelings by denying that there's anything wrong with school – yours or theirs. As homeschooling father and psychotherapist Ken Lipman-Stern says in *GWS* no. 113:

> I ran a men's group for three years. It was a therapy and support group – and I've seen that the toughness of some men is really a wall or a defense system. The man who says, 'My child should have to go through the same tough experiences that I did, because those bad experiences build character', is, I think, holding on to the exterior wall of toughness without examining the pain he felt at going through experiences that were unwanted and harmful.

The solution is grand and beautiful, though perhaps difficult. Unschooling is a statement of faith in human nature. By living your life as proof that you can learn and grow without an institution's control, you show them that they can do the same. If they had childhood interests which they've squelched, it's not too late to reclaim them. If they hate their jobs, they can find ways to replace them with work they love. Don't preach or be condescending to your parents about this, but find ways to support their interests. If your mother says she always wished she had time to plant a flower garden, bring her library books full of flower gardens, or offer to help with planting and weeding.

'I'm afraid you want to be so independent that you won't need me. That makes me feel insecure.' Don't force your parents to say this. Just point out that you value and need their support, that you can't succeed without their blessing, that unschooling helps to destroy barriers in other families and is likely to do so in yours too.

'I'm afraid of what my friends, boss or colleagues will think.' Don't force your parents to bring this one up either; they won't want to sound mundane or insecure when you are discussing the lofty principles of trust, freedom and learning. And, obviously, you mustn't say you know they want you to stay in so that they can avoid shame and embarrassment. That's an accusation, and then they have to defend themselves against you instead of supporting you. (Anyway, you don't know this, any more than they know the inside of your brain.) Instead, take away their fear without ever mentioning it.

Tell your parents about some of the people who have been 'successful' without school, and that unschoolers who want to prepare for college have no real trouble with admissions in most countries. You could agree to use terminology that your parents find comfortable – perhaps 'doing independent study' rather than something brash like 'unschooling' or, God forbid, 'dropping out'. If you are college bound, tell your parents they can say so to anyone who asks. (Because the international unschooling movement is still quite young, the first wave of unschoolers in some countries may have a more difficult time with college and university admissions. One of the best ways to negotiate this challenge is to get a diploma from an accredited, recognized international homeschooling institution such as Clonlara – *see* the resource listings in the back of this book.)

Once you are an actual unschooler, keep making it easy for them by being articulate, presentable, funny, intelligent, interesting and expert. That is, as much as you can be these things without compromising yourself. In general, give them every opportunity to be proud of you and the unschooling movement.

BEYOND 'NO'

1 Ask your parents why they said, 'No'. See if you can strike a compromise. Ask them if there's anything you can do that would get them to say 'yes'.
2 Suggest a trial run. You could agree that if they're not satisfied with your way of educating yourself, that you go to school. Of course, the whole idea of being watched and evaluated runs contrary to the idea of pursuing interests because you *want* to. Still, you could probably psyche yourself into it and make it work.
3 Continue to read up on the subject of unschooling and education in general, and keep giving your parents articles and library books.
4 Help them *feel* what you feel. Ask them to attend school with you for a day, and to take notes and do the homework just as if they were students. Or, without sounding threatening, ask them to think about how they want to be treated when *they* are powerless. For example, when they are old do they want you to take their choices seriously, or would they like you to abandon them to a 'nursing home' or other institution?
5 See if any of your parents' friends or relatives can understand your side. If they can, ask them to intervene on your behalf.
6 Ask them again to think hard about their own ways of learning and their own past, and whether they think school was truly good for them, and how much they learned there.
7 Watch *Dead Poets' Society* with them. At heart, it's a film

about unschooling; at heart, unschooling is all about 'seizing the day'.

8 If you can, survive spiritually by focusing more on your life outside school and not worrying too much about your grades.

9 When you sense the timing is right, ask them to reconsider.

BEYOND 'YES'

After they say 'yes', you want to live with them in harmony. Try to be tolerant of your parents' worries, especially at first. If they are a bit overbearing, don't panic – they'll relax. If they ask you to study in a fairly rigid way at first, try to co-operate – many unschooling families start this way and then slowly come to their senses, abandoning unnecessary structure.

If your parents just can't relax, find yourself an adult advisor, mentor or tutor who understands unschooling and whom your parents respect. Chances are, once they see that this adult doesn't get worked up over your choices, they'll back off.

If they *still* watch you too closely, turn the tables on them with a friendly (if possible) sense of humor. Watch them back. Take notes on how well they seem to be learning, and how well they use what they learn. Give them progress reports. Once they get the message, stop.

Most importantly, continue to do all you can to support and encourage *their* dreams. If your independence inspires them to change their own lives dramatically, don't freak out. Stand behind them and beam.

10 | The Not Necessarily Difficult Legal Issue

Homeschooling is clearly legal in all 50 states of the US and in many other countries, and each year the laws get better. Though the legalities could still stand a lot of improvement, growing numbers of people support homeschooling. When homeschoolers are so obviously living intelligently and happily, and when their average test scores are higher than school students' average test scores – even though these tests narrowly reflect mainly *school* methods of learning – legislators and courts look rather silly requiring them to go back to school 'for their own good'. Truth is on your side.

This chapter will give you some basic pointers and information on the legal aspects of homeschooling. Yes, I am shifting my terminology a little. In this chapter, I will mostly use the euphemism 'homeschooling' rather than 'unschooling'. Unschooling is not a legally recognized term, and probably never will be. Don't use it when you talk to schools, courts or legislators.

('Homeschooling' or 'home educating' implies that *somebody* is teaching you, even if it's 'only' your parents. That's easier for arrogant professional educators to swallow. Of course, you *do* have guiding adults in your life, but no one should be bossing you about. Gradually, tactfully, start letting people know that you are responsible for your own education. But don't strut around acting as if you don't need no help from nobody. It's not true, and it will earn you enemies.)

Note The information in this chapter is as accurate as I could make it. However, it is not intended as *official* legal advice, which I am not qualified to give.

WHAT THE LAWS SAY

Laws about homeschooling vary widely throughout the world. Generally speaking, they're best and most clear in the US, and homeschoolers in many other countries work to get their laws changed to resemble American laws. In the US, however, laws are different in every state. And even within each state, separate districts have varying policies and attitudes.

Most statutes specify that you must register, be in 'homeschool' for a certain number of days and a certain number of hours, and that you keep attendance records. Some statutes ask that you keep records such as logs, portfolios of written work, and even written evaluations of progress; in some areas, you must show these records to certain officials. (Be creative with unsavory regulations. If your state or country requires a progress report, write it yourself and have your parents sign it.) None of these requirements should cause problems. Attendance in school can certainly include educational field trips, such as your kayaking expedition around the Greek islands.

Another common requirement is that parents provide instruction in the same areas school do – mathematics, English, science, art, history, health, etc. Don't panic when you read this stipulation. By pursuing your interests, you will automatically include some of these subjects. On the leftover ones, you can either leave them out and probably not get caught, or else you can study them in a way that you find interesting. There are so many ways to explore any subject that you can almost certainly end up with a legal program that you like, even if it includes subjects you used to hate. See the rest of this book for ways to design a program you can love and everyone else can accept.

And remember: laws rarely ask you to imitate school *methods* – like textbooks, marks, grades or reports. School activities take most of their shape from rigid schedules, bureaucratic logistics and limited access to the outside world. There's no point in lowering your intellect to that level.

Other requirements may be more bothersome:

1 Because people just don't get it about self-education and insist on believing that homeschoolers are taught by their parents, some statutes say a lot about parents' qualifications. In some parts of the US, for instance, one parent must hold a high school diploma or GED diploma. In others, a university degree is required. In a few states, if neither of your parents has a teaching certificate, you must consult occasionally with a certified teacher. Sometimes, these states pay for this by technically enrolling you in school and paying a teacher–consultant.

2 Some states and countries require you to take standardized tests, either once a year or once every few years. In other areas, you are required to submit some type of annual 'assessment'. Standardized testing is one of your choices, but you can also elect an alternative method, such as having a certified teacher evaluate your progress, or assembling a portfolio of your work. Still other states and countries have no assessment requirements at all.

STRATEGIES

The best way to find out how things really work, and what's really allowed, is to contact a local homeschooling organization. These groups can share the lessons learned by all their members and contacts. They have had experience dealing with local laws and school officials, and can offer you invaluable advice. Many groups even publish legal guides. You can find groups near you by contacting one of the organizations in your country, listed below. The annual Directory issue of *GWS* (*see* below and Appendix) is another good way to find out about groups all over the world.

One simple way to deal with bothersome legal requirements is to enroll in a long-distance umbrella school. Unlike correspondence schools, umbrella schools usually encourage you to learn as creatively and independently as you wish. They do not provide set curriculums or correspondence teachers; their function is mainly to help you keep records, which usually lead to a diploma, and to handle communications with your local school officials when necessary. (The better programs, like Clonlara, do also give good advice when you ask for it. *See* below and Appendix for more information.) Usually, an umbrella school charges a flat fee for the services it provides each family. If it solves your legal worries and thus sets you free, it's money very well spent.

AN OUNCE OF PREVENTION

If you use a bit of diplomacy, you probably won't actually have to deal with hostile school boards, officials or courts. Legal technicalities, after all, are not the only factors which affect your right to homeschool; unspoken social rules are even more important and fundamental. The following suggestions are especially important if you live in one of the states or countries where people have to request permission to homeschool. However, they can help maintain peace and goodwill anywhere.

Trust, as much as you can. Don't turn a peaceful situation into a war. Until they prove otherwise, assume that the local schoolpeople are your allies. Assume that they want you to have the best possible education, and that therefore they will cheer you on. Teachers and even administrators will probably support you unless you put them on the defensive.

Most of the teenagers I heard from said they'd never been hassled, and that the schools basically ignored them as long as they fulfilled requirements. In most cases this involved little more than sending in a short statement every September outlining their plans. Some reported that the local schools were not just neutral, but helpful and supportive. Thirteen-year-old Anne Brosnan, for instance, wrote, 'The school is perfectly happy with us, and we've never been to court. About twice a year a lady comes from Babylon Schools to visit us, and she's really nice and we like her. We don't take tests and she just makes sure we are pretty "smart"!'

Understand what the schoolpeople have to lose: money and pride. Don't carelessly say or do things that increase their losses.

Money: if you quit by the dozens or hundreds, teachers and other schoolpeople will panic about their jobs, reasonably enough.

Pride: quite aside from the homeschooling movement, the teaching profession has long suffered from a general feeling of not being respected or taken seriously enough. Teachers in the US and many other parts of the world do face injustice – they are not trusted with enough independence or creativity in the classroom, they are swamped with inane clerical details, students and parents viciously blame them for things that are beyond their control, and their pay is low compared with other careers that require similar qualifications. All this discourages teachers from living with healthy humility and honesty; instead, it encourages them to be generally defensive and too concerned with their reputations.

To teachers of this unfortunate mentality, homeschooling feels like an additional slap in the face, even a challenge to do battle. After they wear themselves out convincing the public that they are knowledgeable, indispensable professionals, homeschooling families come along and say, 'We don't need you. Our kids will have better educations without you.'

(Of course, there are many earnest teachers with self-esteem intact enough to see clearly. They are not puffed up with superficial pride, and will be glad to see you escape to learn freely, even though they may nevertheless worry about their jobs.)

Teachers' money and pride panics are not your fault; they are the natural and fitting consequences of an arrogant profession which preys on the planet's young. However, you may want to do something to alleviate the problem for them. With tact, you can make things easier for both you and the schoolpeople, at least in the short term. If you want to ease the money panic, in some states and countries you can find a way to stay partially enrolled in school so they get their pay (chapter 16). If you want to ease the pride panic, you can avoid making public statements that accuse teachers of incompetence. In your conversations, focus instead on the structural problems of schools, and point out that the system prevents teachers from teaching to their best ability. No honest teacher will disagree with you there.

FREE THE PLANET!

If you live in one of the countries where unschooling is difficult, lucky you. Yours is the chance to make history. You may have to fortify yourself with a bottle of courage vitamins, but your actions are truly important. Your example will open the door so a big blast of fresh air can blow into the brains of your friends and classmates.

The unschooling movement in many countries – especially in the Western world – largely resembles that of the US in the 1970s and 1980s. That is, there are few homeschoolers, so they feel more isolated. Laws are generally more ambiguous, and there are proportionally fewer unschooling *teenagers*. It's my guess that in 10 or 20 years, the numbers, laws and attitudes in these countries will increase and improve dramatically, just as they have in the US. That makes for a hopeful vision, and you can help make it come true.

When a law is unclear, homeschoolers attempt to interpret the law as it applies to them. In some ways this ambiguity can be a blessing – that is, a law may not state that homeschooling is allowed, but neither does it explicitly prohibit homeschooling. Usually, though, homeschoolers prefer to push for specific legislation, hoping that this will clearly establish their rights. The US has gone through this process during the past 20 years. There are still a few states where homeschooling rights are a bit fuzzy, but that doesn't stop people from doing what they believe in.

In most regions of most English-speaking countries, it's legal to homeschool, and there is a thriving, rapidly growing unschooling movement, with numerous support groups, a few nationwide organizations and newsletters. (The terms 'deschooling' or 'natural learning' are used more than 'unschooling'. Also, like in the US, many people use the terms 'homeschooling' and 'home-education' to mean self-directed education.) Barbara J Smith, who directs the Calgary Montessori Home Education Program in Alberta, Canada, gives advice which is realistic for teenagers in most English-speaking countries:

> Take advantage of the flexibility. Find a mentor or an apprenticeship. Do job shadowing. Let your program be interest based – you can't do it all. Aim for good research skills, good critical thinking skills. Be entrepreneurial. Value informal leaning. Look in your own community. Travel when you can.

Have fun learning. Learn a foreign language – go there!

Within our program, I facilitate special projects for teenage students – such as work experience in an eye clinic, construction and decoration of a family room, travel in Greece with interviews of relatives and documenting the sites, an equestrian project training a miniature horse, food studies and menu design.

In most European countries, it is legal or semi-legal to homeschool but still rare, somewhat difficult, and often frowned upon. Katherine Hebert is a 14-year-old who holds both Swiss and American citizenship. Her unschooling experiences reflect those of many Europeans:

> Once you've settled in and have sunk into routine, you realize [that homeschooling in Switzerland] has quite a few advantages. The main one is that you are in the centre of Europe, culture capital of the world. To make my point I'll give you a few statistics: if you aren't scared to fly and have an extra 200 dollars saved up from the last bake sale, why not go to Stockholm? How about Russia? Turkey? Greece? England? The places are limitless. The Italian border is four hours away by train (considering I can't drive yet I take the train everywhere), Rome five and Venice six. Germany is an hour and a half, the French border twenty minutes and Paris two hours. Get the picture? Only two weeks ago I was doing volunteer work in Sarajevo, Bosnia, a half-hour plane trip away ...
>
> The resources are more difficult to get than in the States. The local library is only accessible to adults, my mother's World Health Organization library is only for WHO workers and the US embassy library only for embassy workers. I get around this problem by posing as an 18-year-old at the local library, as my mother at the WHO library, and as a secretary at the embassy under a fake name; I hope they never actually check to see if I work there. I also get a lot of my information off the Net.
>
> If someone is interested in homeschooling here, I think it's a great idea. If you have a strong drive for learning and like to get out and do stuff this is the perfect place for you.

There's little information available on unschooling in most parts of Africa, Asia and Central and South America. That doesn't mean it's not happening – undoubtedly, there are young autodidacts in every nation, though they may feel totally alone and not realize they're part of a worldwide movement. If you live in an area where no one has heard of unschooling, it's truly up to you to be the bright ray of brave hope. Aleta Shepler's advice for unschooling teenagers in Venezuela could be well adapted to most of South America and, in fact, to much of the world:

> If you are interested in a traditional book-centred type of home education, you will need a lot of money for such an endeavor in Venezuela. There are public libraries, but you can't take out the books. You can use the Internet now but sometimes the phone system doesn't work and in the interior the electricity only works for certain hours of the day. However, if you are interested in experiential education, there is a great deal of freedom and opportunity to explore your passion.
>
> Our children have observed capuchin monkeys in their native environment, interviewed Bolivian women regarding their traditional strategies for family planning, worked with street kids, directed a neighborhood theatre group, built a recycling center, studied the impact of subsistence farming on the rainforest, learned to write a proposal, a petition, and make power phone calls, run an import comic book business, learned to ride and train a horse, raised rabbits and dogs, trained a parrot, etc ... They have learned a great deal about cross-cultural conflict resolution.
>
> If you learn best with a mentor, there are many possibilities. In the capital city, there are many artisans who can serve as mentors in ceramics, clothing design and construction, carving, painting, etc.With the help of an agent there are opportunities in theater, movies and commercials ... In the interior, there are still people who can show you how to build a grass roof, carve a canoe, observe and identify the flora and fauna of the rainforest.
>
> Most of the kinds of activities which are extra-curricular but

school related in the US (such as sports, music, drama and art) are done in social clubs in Venezuela. For example, our daughter Halee belongs to a horse club and spends every afternoon riding with her Venezuelan friends. Our son Os attends a comic art institute every morning, where he meets with his mentor and shares his work and imported comic books with his fellow learners (ranging in age from 18 to 48).

I would highly recommend that you design your home-based educational endeavor around a big problem or question that needs to be solved. Venezuela is a country which is in crisis and it is our family's experience that you can learn most academic subjects and many skills by making the resolution of a social problem the focus of your study. Our children have devoted 85 percent of their educational budget to social problem-solving expeditions. We believe that this is the true meaning of 'public education'.

While there are many opportunities and legal freedoms in Venezuela for homeschoolers, it is not always easy. You will have to develop the skills of a detective to sniff out mentors, apprenticeships and other learning resources. And you will have many well-meaning Venezuelans and expatriates who will try to direct you to traditional schooling. Non-conventional education in Venezuela is for risk-takers, social change agents and the passionate. It is not for followers or the faint of heart.

GENERAL RESOURCES

- *Growing Without Schooling* magazine (*see* Appendix) publishes frequent articles on international home-schooling and lists homeschooling organizations around the world.
- The annual Directory issue of *GWS* (*see* Appendix) is updated frequently and includes the latest addresses for dozens of international homeschooling organizations.
- Clonlara's Home Based Education Program (*see* Appendix). If you are not sure about the laws in your

country, or if homeschooling seems to be illegal or semi-legal, or if you'd simply like some long-distance support, enroll with Clonlara. These people are amazing! They provide a legal structure for homeschoolers in 20 countries so far, as well as in all 50 states of the US. They are expert at dealing with school officials all over the world, and have even been able to help people homeschool in Germany and Japan, two of the most difficult countries for unschoolers. Very few of their client families outside the US are American citizens.

The Internet

Search for 'homeschooling' and you'll find heaps of information pertaining to many countries. Jon Shemitz's and Karl Bunday's Web sites (*see* Appendix) provide worldwide information and link to other international sites. Also see:

• The Homeschooling Zone (includes a worldwide directory of homeschoolers), www.caro.net/~joespa/
• The Canadian Alliance of Homeschoolers (good worldwide links), www.netroute.net/~altpress/ds/cahs.html

THE COUNTRIES

Please note that I list only each country's largest or broadest organizations, but these can put you in touch with smaller groups near you. Almost all these organizations are run completely by volunteers – sometimes it's just one dedicated family. So when you write, be sure to include a large self-addressed envelope with stamps or international reply coupons, and it's also nice to send a little money to cover photocopying costs. If no organization is listed for your country, you may be able to find one via the general resources listed above – and, no matter where you live, Clonlara can probably help you homeschool legally.

What if your country isn't listed? I don't have information about homeschooling everywhere, and I don't have room here, anyway, to go into detail on all the countries that I do know about. In addition to the countries discussed below, I have heard from and about home-schoolers in Bermuda, Brazil, Haiti, Israel, Mexico, Nigeria, the Philippines, Portugal, Russia, Saudi Arabia, Sri Lanka, Taiwan and the West Indies (Jamaica). Do your best to find other homeschoolers – again, the resources above will help. Or just sniff out the local laws and give it your best shot. Then, write and tell me about your adventures so I can talk about them in the next edition of this book!

Those living abroad form a large, though dispersed, homeschooling community. Military families have practically no problem homeschooling anywhere – even in Germany – and most other expatriates have no problem in most countries. Valerie Bonham Moon, an American in Germany, says that 'any military personnel can consult DoD Manual 1342.6-M, and also read UR 10–12.' She is beginning to form a network of military families homeschooling abroad, and you can contact her at HQs USAREUR, CMR 420, Box 606, APO AE 09063, starrmoon@hotmail.com.

Australia

Despite – or because of? – difficult laws in some states and territories, Australia has a thriving, though small, com-munity of homeschoolers who are politically active and alert. Officials and number-people put the total at somewhere between 5,000 and 20,000 among the country's population of 18 million. 'As in the US,' says Janine Banks of New South Wales, 'there are restrictive laws in a couple of states, but many people continue to home educate as they wish. To the best of my knowledge, no one has ever been jailed for home educating in Australia ... Most of the general population do not know it is a legal alternative to school, and there is a lack of awareness of home education and its advantages. This means there are very few resources specifically for home educators and most of the support literature I have read comes from the US or Britain. We are a growing movement but still in our infancy.'

The worst state is Queensland where, if your parents aren't registered teachers, they're supposed to hire one to teach you or else enroll you in a correspondence school. Yet, at least 200 homeschooling families – in Brisbane alone – do not comply with these regulations; it seems that most Queensland homeschoolers simply don't bother to notify the authorities, and they get away with it. Eleanor Sparks remarks in her Web page, 'The Education Department seems to be putting a lot of the homeschooling issues into the "too hard" basket.' If you want to unschool yourself in Queensland, you should definitely get in touch with a local homeschooling group, and *not* with the Education Department. At the other end of the Australian legal spectrum is Victoria and the Australian Capital Territories, where the law clearly allows people to homeschool without permission from the Education Department.

The other states and territories at least seem to have more homeschoolers than rules and regulations *about* homeschooling. Jo-Anne Beirne of Homeschoolers Australia Pty Ltd writes in *GWS* no. 101:

> The lack of national approach to education has been good for homeschooling ... Because some states do not have a process for certifying that a student has completed high school, access to jobs has not traditionally been predicated on the school examination process, but rather on workplace examinations and interviews.

Further information

- Homeschoolers Australia Pty Ltd, PO Box 420, Kellyville NSW 2153, tel. 02 6293727
- Eleanor Sparks's wonderful and funny Australian Home Schooling Resource Page, www.3dproductions.com.au/homeschool/
- The Australian Home Education Page, http://cs.anu. edu.au/people/Drew.Corrigan/home_ed/overview.html

Belgium

Karen Maxwell, mother of 10- and 14-year-olds in Belgium, runs a small discussion group in Brussels. She reports:

> The biggest difference between the situation in Belgium and that in countries or states that require planned lessons or testing at the end of the school year is that I have *no* restrictions to follow and we 'unschool' rather than follow lesson plans.
>
> Homeschooling is a legal option in Brussels, but it is a fairly well-kept secret. A family who wants to homeschool runs the risk of hearing that it is not legal from a variety of sources that should be reliable. I write a letter to the school inspector of my district once a year for each of my two boys, stating that I take the responsibility for their education for the coming school year. For the last five years, that has been the extent of my contact with the educational establishment.
>
> As there is no legal restriction on homeschooling, the individual school inspector seems to sometimes feel obligated to 'interpret' the law and the reasonable restrictions. I have also known families that had their family allowance stopped, as someone who handled their benefits felt that family allowance was only provided if the children attended school, but in both cases the money was paid after legal proceedings.
>
> All my community contacts know that I homeschool, and I have not been secretive about it and have had no trouble. It is

an option that is used by a very small minority here, and I have no idea what the statistics are. By contrast, in France the option is much better known, although the percentage of home-schoolers may not be much higher than here.

Canada

Each province and territory has its own laws governing homeschooling, and as I write the official count of homeschoolers is about 10,000. British Columbia has the best legal climate for unschooling, with a vital, warm 'deschooling' community; I met dozens of very inde-pendent, bright unschooling teenagers during my speaking trips to Vancouver and Victoria. Homeschoolers must register with a government school, through correspondence courses or with an independent school of their choice. These institutions receive a small amount of money from the government, and in return they provide some resources for the homeschoolers.

Nova Scotia, Alberta and Saskatchewan are pretty good places too. Alberta is similar to British Columbia in that homeschoolers are supposed to register with a school board; they can register with any board in the province. Registered Albertans also receive a small amount of cash for learning supplies.

Laws have improved considerably in the past few years in Ontario, so that school boards no longer have much authority over homeschoolers. Each year, Manitobans must register, submit an educational plan, and then submit two progress reports. Quebec is 'way down near the bottom of the list' when it comes to a good legal climate, with an ambiguous, indefinite law that allows hostile school boards to cause a bit of pain and suffering. Some families stay underground and choose to have nothing to do with the Commission Scolaire; many others enroll with Clonlara or other long-distance umbrella 'schools'. Nevertheless, homeschooling is clearly legal and parents do not need to be certified teachers.

Further information

- The Canadian Homeschool Resource Page (outstanding and comprehensive), www.flora.org/homeschool-ca/
- The Canadian Alliance of Home Schoolers, 272 Hwy #5, RR 1, St George, ON N0E 1N0. tel. 519 448 4001, www.netroute.net/~altpress/ds/cahs.html.
- Virtual High and the WonderTree Education Society, PO Box 380, Vancouver, BC V5Z 4L9, tel. 604 739 5941, http://bc-education.botany.ubc.ca/vh/vh.html. (These are outstanding 'independent schools' that truly serve unschoolers – a great choice for British Columbians.)
- The Calgary Montessori Home Education Program, Community Connections, 101 Point Drive, NW, Calgary, AB T3B 5C8. (For Albertans, this is an excellent program – it's affiliated with a school district and fulfills legal registration requirements, but the director, Barbara J Smith, has many years' experience of unschooling with her own family.)

France

Homeschooling in France is a little-known option, but explicitly legal since 1882. Your family needs only to announce your decision to homeschool two weeks before the new school year starts. You give one declaration to the mayor of your town, and another to the inspector of the regional academy which represents the board of education. The 'authorities' may look into a home-schooler's education at ages 8, 10 and 12, and the academies can require a detailed description of how you plan to reach academic goals. Sophie Haesen, of Alsace, reports that 'In France, usually the first reaction to the fact that homeschooling is legal is surprise and disbelief, even with teachers ... I know of about 200 families who are homeschooling in France, because they are members of the homeschooling network. How many "independent" homeschoolers there are, I do not know, and it is almost impossible to estimate.'

Further information

* Les Enfants d'Abord, c/o Shosha, 4 rue de League, F-34800 Brignac, tel. 33 4 67 96 90 44
(Alternative address: c/o Grde Rue, Valence 26000.)

Germany

The bad news: in early 1997 Germany is the only nation I know of where homeschooling is definitely illegal. Foreign military families are exempt, but all school-aged Germans and non-military foreigners are required to attend school. A few families have homeschooled and fought hard for their right to do so, but have been so harassed that they eventually fled the country. The good news: Clonlara can help even Germans homeschool, through its connections with German alternative schools.

Further information

* Valerie Bonham Moon (from an American military family), HQs USAREUR, CMR 420, Box 606, APO AE 09063, starrmoon@hotmail.com.

New Zealand

There are about 5,000 to 7,000 homeschoolers in New Zealand. This accounts for more than 1 percent of the school-age population, so homeschooling is definitely well known and increasingly popular. Your parents do have to fill out some detailed forms, outline how they intend to address various subjects, and then provide annual reports. Homeschooling mother Debbie Bennett says, 'I don't think the laws are particularly restrictive. As long as you tell the authorities what they want to hear you can be fairly relaxed in your approach. It's up to the individual really – just so long as you appear to play their game.' Homeschooling families receive several hundred dollars each year for educational supplies. Jan Brownlie says, 'It is very easy for teenagers to homeschool, especially if you apply for an exemption [from enrollment at school] and emphasize the work experience angle. In fact, if a teenager over 14 or 15 can say they have a job, they can leave without applying for an exemption.' Jill Whitmore of Auckland notes that:

> It is accepted that children may learn informally as well as formally ... Our own teenagers were able to attend a local school part time during the later part of their homeschooling careers; this was by agreement with the principal and teachers. Some other teenage homeschoolers that we know of have enjoyed similar arrangements.

Further information

- Homeschooling Federation of New Zealand, PO Box 41 226, St Lukes, Auckland
- New Zealand Home Schoolers' Association (NZHSA), PO Box 41–226 St Lukes, Auckland, tel./fax (09) 849 4780

Ireland

The Irish constitution says that the family is the main educator, so homeschooling has long been legal and relatively problem free. It is a growing trend. In *GWS* no. 84 (1991) Mary Delmage Sheehan writes: 'Now that we are starting to organize a homeschooling group, the full extent of homeschooling is becoming apparent and it is clear that it has been going on quietly and successfully for many years ... The reaction of school-going children to homeschooled children usually seems to be, "Lucky things!" and the reaction from adults is similar – "Good idea".'

Further information

- Sa Baile, c/o Theresa Murphy, Clahane, Ballard, Tralee, Co Kerry
- or c/o Marguerite Egan, Cillmhicadomhnaigh, Ventry, Co Kerry

Japan

Thanks to an incredibly stressful and abusive system, around 180,000 'school refusers' between the ages of 6 and 15 have stopped going to school. Because Japan places a high value on schooling, these kids suffer greatly, and they have little or no support for their attempts at saving themselves. Dr Pat Montgomery, director of Clonlara, says:

> Last year the suicide rate of young boys hit an all time high ... When school refusers stop going to school, there are not many places they can go. Their self-esteem sinks to a low because they are disgracing their families ... I must emphasize that they do not make this decision gleefully; they are usually physically ill leading up to it and afterwards ... I was shown a

hospital in Tokyo where all ten floors held children with school phobia ... The idea was to rehabilitate them so that they could go back to school.

Fortunately, a few people have responded with compassion, setting up 'free schools' to help school refusers meet and learn outside the system, and the government has basically averted its eyes. This brave beginning has led to interest in homeschooling also, though many Japanese mistakenly confuse school refusers with homeschoolers.

In 1994, 889 people attended a full-day Tokyo symposium on homeschooling featuring Pat Montgomery. In 1997, Clonlara enrolled 150 families and opened a Japanese office in Kyoto, with a Japanese contact teacher, Konomi Shinohara Corbin. This program is adapted for the needs of Japanese homeschoolers, which differ in some ways from those in other countries. 'Now is the time for homeschooling to wax,' says Pat, 'while its existence is officially ignored by the powers that be. Another case of "When the people lead, the leaders follow."'

Of course, being *allowed* to homeschool is only half the battle in Japan. Whether a homeschooler will grow up and be accepted as an adult member of Japanese society remains to be seen. 'There may be a serious risk of not having access to higher education, or problems getting a job without the junior high school graduation certificate,' writes Kyoko Aizawa of Otherwise Japan. She reports that the Japanese advisory panel for education recently proposed that school refusers and homeschoolers should be allowed to take an exam in order to receive that certificate, but they would still not be able to say on their résumés that they had actually graduated from junior high school. Kyoko, lawyer Sayoko Ishii, and other homeschooling advocates are hoping instead for better legislation that clearly allows and recognizes homeschooling as a worthy path into responsible adulthood, and they feel that equivalency exams are not the answer. In the meantime, Clonlara has some helpful news:

> Several of our Japanese students have graduated with our Clonlara diploma and have entered colleges and universities there – even the renowned Waseda University. So, we have no problems on that score. Others have used their Clonlara credentials to go into the workforce or to do television and theatre work.

At this point, Clonlara students may still have to take Japanese exams to earn their graduation certificates, but at least they can prepare for those exams outside of the school system. 'The legal position of homeschooling is unclear,' says Leslie Barson in *GWS* no. 106, 'and until this is clarified, the present homeschoolers are frightened and cannot join together. Nor can they advertise homeschooling as a choice for Japanese families.' Of course, since compulsory schooling stops at age 15, theoretically it's possible for older teenagers to find some way to take charge of their educations outside the system, but independent learners cannot necessarily expect to be accepted by employers or universities.

Further information

• Otherwise Japan, PO Box Kugayama, Suginami-ku, Tokyo, JAB02521@niftyserve.or.jp.

The Netherlands

Homeschooling is legal, but not well known; it took one mother almost six years to track down information. In 1988, a homeschooling family won an important court case, partly through proving their seriousness (they said they'd leave the country if the child was forced to attend school). In *GWS* no.102, Liz Meyer Groenveld writes about her seven-year-old daughter:

> My worries have always been about the higher grades. Academic standards are very high here; for example, to enter university, one must know not only Dutch but English, German and French. And in Holland one must have a trade diploma even for work such as flower arranging ... But reading *GWS* never fails to reassure me that where there's a will, there's a way. I think that as long as we can meet the academic requirements, Lizzy should have no more trouble passing a state exam to enter university here than any transfer student from another country would have. Now that she is ... quite fluent in English and Dutch, I am working on finding someone to teach her German ... I plan to ensure that Lizzy can homeschool as long as she wants to ... I do think people assume that we are doing things very officially, with tutors and textbooks, when in fact we are unschooling. I also ask the schoolchildren regularly what they're working on, and in most areas we're way ahead of Lizzy's class despite the minuscule amount of time we set aside for actual lessons.

Further information

- Netherlands Homeschoolers, Raadhuislaan 31, 2131 Hoofddoorp
- The Alternative Learning Exchange, http://mcs.nl/ale/ale-3.html#contents

South Africa

The homeschooling movement here is alive and kicking. The old government vehemently opposed homeschooling and the present parliament is not exactly eager to dispense freedom either. But with the new, more democratic government, activists *have* won major improvements – and continue to fight for more. Our star is Kate Durham, who says, 'I was your average housewife except that I knew what had to be done and how to do it.' Kate organized an association, helped motivate homeschoolers in other provinces to organize as well, and then traveled repeatedly to Cape Town to educate politicians.

As a result of her work and that of other dedicated people, South Africa now has national legislation which allows homeschooling, though you still have to register and then hope that the government will grant approval. Many families homeschool openly without registering, though, somewhat fortified by a growing public resistance to state interference in private matters. How many homeschoolers? 'A guesstimate puts the figure at about 1,300 ... with the majority underground,' says Kate. 'Our association's membership grew close to 100 percent in 1996.' The state schools are terrible, and the private schools are expensive, so Kate expects the trend to continue. (Ironically and obnoxiously, the old South African compulsory school laws did not apply to black kids. In a letter to *GWS*, Kate says, 'White children were herded into schools. It is my personal belief that this was an effective way of perpetuating the myths and fears on which apartheid survived.')

Further information

- National Coalition of Home Schoolers, PO Box 14, Dundee, 3000, tel. 0341 23712, durham@liadun.dundee. lia.net.

Spain

The laws are ambiguous, but homeschoolers are pretty much allowed to do as they please; as Bippan Norberg points out, the law 'has basically been used to force poor families to bring their kids to school instead of using them as labor'. In fact, in once court case a judge condemned 150 such families, but said later that the problem was not the lack of schooling per se – it was a larger issue of neglect and abuse. He said that legal consequences would probably *not* apply to homeschoolers, because 'in a case like that, the parents do not let go of their obligations towards their children, but the opposite – they take responsibility for choosing the best educational method for their children'.

As far as Bippan knows, no family has had serious legal problems with homeschooling, and there is a nationwide homeschooling movement of at least a few hundred families. 'But we know that a lot more people would do it if it was completely legal,' she says. 'Lots don't even know it is semi-legal. Some families are completely open about it, like we are, and have not had any problems at all ... Others do it completely in secret and are afraid. From our point of view they are afraid of things that they absolutely have no reason to be afraid of.' Bippan and her family hold national meetings for homeschoolers, most of them week-long camps, and usually about 50 people attend. They also send out an information pack on request.

Bippan's 15-year-old son, Lomi Szil, is one of few teenage homeschoolers in Spain. Most of his friends hate school, but do not see homeschooling as an alternative for themselves since they've never had much chance to decide *anything* for themselves. Lomi says that if any Spanish teenagers *do* choose to homeschool, there are plenty of opportunities to take courses and try out all kinds of things. 'Even when the rules say that you have to be a certain age or show that you are at school, here in Spain you can always get round the rules. Many courses have a lower age limit of 16 of 18, but only because there is nobody under that age who *can* take part, since they are all at school. Despite the lack of unschooling peers, Lomi manages to educate himself with amazing vitality. Among other things, he juggles, contemplates going to circus school, studies aikido, is a boy scout, plays basketball, has his own business selling organic popcorn at festivals, volunteers for Greenpeace, organizes festivals with his mother, and is starting a food cooperative with friends, where he hopes to cook vegetarian meals.

Further information

- Crecer Sin Escuela, c/o Norberg-Szil, Apdo 45, E-03580 l'Alfás del Pi, Alicante

Switzerland

Local authorities have some power over your choices, and only a tiny handful of people have chosen to homeschool, let alone *un*school. Essentially, some parts of the country allow homeschooling, and others don't. Homeschooler Marie Heitzmann reports that Ticino is the worst place: 'When people from there want to homeschool, I tell them to move.' In the Vaud canton, where Marie lives, and in Geneva, homeschoolers have to take a fairly simple exam each year. Fourteen-year-old Katherine Hebert, an American with dual citizenship, reports that:

> Homeschooling is not really encouraged in Switzerland and to tell the truth homeschooling is more or less considered by the Swiss and French as something of a hippie movement, associated with high school dropouts and drugs. The only children who are informed of their right to homeschool are those with two or three hours commuting to and from school,

where homeschooling is considered to be "beneficial" to their education (implying that in other circumstances it isn't beneficial). Swiss students inquiring into homeschooling have doors slammed in their faces; the people are kept ignorant of the educational possibilities ...

Yet, homeschooling is legal under Swiss law if you follow the rules, although these rules restrict homeschoolers and keep them within neat boundaries. I enrolled in Clonlara, which is mainly a school on paper. I have practically nil correspondence with them and am left free to my studies. I have an exceptionally open-minded school district officer, who after a few Sundays over at our home to have tea and cakes, warmed to the homeschooling idea and then gave me full support, offering tutoring, classes at the Swiss school, and great project ideas.

Ironically, the very rigidity of the school system in Switzerland makes it easy for *teenagers* to homeschool, even without their parents' approval. As in many European countries, the schools are based on a tracking system. Uninterested students finish when they are 14 or 15, and then usually go into apprenticeships. Though this rigid system certainly has its drawbacks – the Swiss suicide rate is the world's second highest, and the apprenticeship track is low status – at least it also provides a loophole through which fed-up teenagers can escape. As Marie points out, 'Most Swiss parents would not accept homeschooling, but would have no choice if the kid didn't have the grades to stay in school.'

Further information

Marie is willing for you to contact her at Au Village 12, 1277 Borex. She also suggests contacting the French organization, Les Enfants D'Abord, at Relations Internationales, Claudia Gringmann, impasse Jean Pierre,

66130 Trevillach, France, or at the address listed under 'France'. If enough Swiss are interested, Marie says she will consider forming a Swiss organization, though her traveling schedule may prevent her from doing so immediately.

United Kingdom

Homeschooling is unquestionably legal and well established throughout the United Kingdom. Roland Meighan, director of Education Now, estimates about 20,000 to 25,000 teenagers, but other homeschooling leaders guess under 1,000. Some people feel it's easier to homeschool in the UK than in the US – the regulations are the same throughout the whole country, and therefore easier to communicate and understand. Few people homeschool for religious reasons, so British homeschoolers don't quarrel much among themselves. Formal testing is not required. Homeschoolers do not have to follow the National Curriculum. And homeschoolers *can* take GCSEs and 'A' level exams at home.

On the minus side, school officials have the right to visit homeschoolers to ensure that their education is 'suitable' to the 'age, ability, aptitude and any special educational need' of the learner, and in a few areas these visits are intrusive and aggressive. It's difficult to attend school part time in Britain, though on that front the visionary Roland Meighan is working to raise awareness and bring about many improvements. He advocates 'flexi-schooling', sort of a combination of homeschooling and using schools part time. Finally, at this point it may be harder for homeschoolers to gain admittance to universities in the UK than in the US, but homeschoolers *have* been admitted to Cambridge, Oxford and York universities.

Further information

- Education Otherwise, PO Box 7420, London N9 9SG, tel. 01926 886828, www.educate.co.uk/edother.htm
- Education Now, 113 Arundel Drive, Bramcote Hills, Nottingham NG9 3FQ, tel. 0115 925 7261
- Home Education Advisory Service, PO Box 98, Welwyn Garden City, Herts. AL8 6AN, http://ourworld. compuserve.com/homepages/home_ed_advisory_srv
- Advice for Home Educators in England and Wales, www.educate.co.uk/leainfo.htm.

United States

In most respects and in most states, it is easy for US citizens to unschool. Unschooling teenagers in some areas still feel rather isolated, and the laws could still do with some major improvements but, compared with the situation of the 1970s and the 1980s, there are few problems. (It makes sense that US citizens have it the easiest, considering that's where the homeschooling movement started.)

Education laws are the business of each state, not of the federal government. Therefore, for example, Californians and Iowans face completely different sets of regulations. Every state has statutes, or written laws, on compulsory education. Most of these laws now have specific provisions for homeschooling.

There are homeschooling groups in every state, and you can communicate by mail if not in person. Some of the groups near you may be so strongly biased towards certain religious or other beliefs that you feel alienated by them. However, even many fundamentalist Christian homeschooling groups are very helpful to less religiously oriented unschoolers. *Don't* ask your school or school board about homeschooling laws. These people are often completely misinformed.

Further information

- Holt Associates, 2269 Massachusetts Ave., Cambridge, MA 02140, tel. 617 864 3100, 76202.3703@compuserve. com.
- Jon Shemitz's 'Jon's Homeschool Resource' page, www. midnightbeach.com/hs/
- Karl M Bunday's 'School is Dead/Learn in Freedom' page, http://198.83.19.39/School_is_dead/Learn_in freedom.html
- The Home Education Press page (includes information on laws in all 50 states of the US), www.home-ed-press.com/wlcm_hsinf.hmtl

Venezuela

The good news: school is not compulsory, and the lower classes have a thriving apprenticeship system. The bad news: social expectations are very, very powerful and, for people who can afford to go to school, it is definitely not acceptable to take charge of your own education. (School is free up until the age of about 14 but nevertheless, many families cannot afford the necessary books, uniforms and supplies.) 'For an upper class family to decide to educate their children at home, using the apprenticeship model, is unthinkable!' reports Aleta Shepler, a US citizen and mother of three unschoolers. Even so, people's minds can change. Aleta says that Venezuelan acquaintances 'were critical of our choice until they saw that Kirsten was able to attend college, Halee was published in a magazine and Os was accepted on to a Venezuelan university art program at age 15. Now there are very few open criticisms.'

11 | The Importance of The Vacation

Before you can start your new way of life, you have to let go of the old one.

There are loud cruel voices you must banish, before you can hear the sweet faint muses. There are harsh schedules you must cancel, before you can coax your natural rhythms back into place.

Learning at school is swimming upstream against the current of your natural curiosity and rhythm. It takes exhausting effort, but it can be done. Unschooling is swimming downstream, still kicking and paddling and crossing over to investigate the shores, but without fighting. If you don't give yourself time to turn round in the river, unschooling will be a miserable confusion. If you don't give yourself time to adjust, this book will not work for you. Still facing upstream, you'll drift downstream. In other words, you'll be neither here nor there ... and maybe you'll end up wanting to be back *there*, in school, because at least there you know where you are.

The vacation I hereby suggest is your time to turn round – and rest – before you make any effort to steer your course. If you don't take a vacation, you may start unschooling with the same frenzied guilty complexes with which you've been schooling.

YOUR VACATION

When you leave school, do nothing academic for at least, at the absolute minimum, a week. If you wish, however, write stories or journal entries about your past and your future. Dream, dream, dream. If you crave TV, watch it. If you crave sleep, indulge. Allow yourself to go through withdrawal. Pass no judgments. If you want to 'work' on anything, work on forgiving and forgetting. Forgive yourself for everything. Forgive your teachers for everything. Forgive your parents for everything. Forget the lies school taught – forget that learning is separate from your life, that you can't teach yourself, that you are defined by your grades, and all other such nonsense. Detoxify. Purge.

Obviously, your parents need to know this vacation is coming. If not, they may anxiously pile textbooks around you and assign essays on 'The Reign of Queen Elizabeth'. I don't know about you, but that sort of well-intentioned concern would certainly drive *me* back to school. If they don't think they can handle watching you do nothing for a week or so, visit your grandmother.

AND AFTER THE VACATION

Unfortunately, I can't promise that all your school wounds will heal in one short week. The complete process of unschooling your spirit could take a month or even years. Anthony J Hermans, 17, reflects, 'It's not easy to learn to deal with freedom – especially when you're used to something else.' Judy Garvey, a homeschooling parent, calls the transition process 'flushing out'. She points out in *GWS* no. 70 that it can involve a period of hating the mention of anything remotely connected to academic work, or even a temporary lack of interest in *everything*.

A few enemies may lurk in your gut, waiting to make life difficult. Fear, for example, may overwhelm you at first. Most of the structure in your world has suddenly evaporated, and not just for the weekend. Your time is yours, and you may feel dazed by the responsibility of it. Expect to be afraid; just don't give in to that fear. Where there's fear, say some wise women I know, there's power. No one feels afraid when they walk into a boring job for the 14th year, which is a sorry reason to do a boring job for 14 years.

Another enemy is the guilt that blocks your natural curiosity. People who have never gone to school have never developed negative attitudes toward exploring their world. Unfortunately, you probably have. It's not your fault if you don't immediately want to run out and watch spiders with a magnifying glass. It might take time before your desire to learn surfaces from beneath the layers of guilt – the voices insisting I *should* learn this, I *have to* learn that. Give yourself that time. Don't push. You'll recover. One unschooler's father told me he thought it would take a year before a new unschooler could do anything 'real' and start going forward on his or her own.

Impatience, too: in chapter 3 I pointed out that schools helped 18th- and 19th-century factory owners by forcing people to shift from a natural, agricultural way of scheduling their lives to an artificial, industrial way. Quitting school, you can ease back into a healthy tempo, but you'll have to be more patient with yourself than factory owners are with their employees. Allow yourself to find a natural pace, even though that means you may slow down, stare into space more often, breathe more easily. You won't necessarily accomplish less – many homeschoolers accomplish far more than their schooled peers – but it's OK if you *do* accomplish less. The meaning of life has to do with quality, not quantity.

The worst thing that can go wrong with your unschooling is lack of trust.

If your parents don't trust you, they will nag or look like they want to nag. If they see you watching TV they may assume that's all you'll ever do. It will drive you crazy. You'll wish you were back at school, where everyone expects you not to want to learn anything. Tell them how important their trust is. Continue to educate them about homeschooling. Share the stories in this chapter with them. Introduce them to other unschooling families through your local groups.

If the school board doesn't trust you, that's not so bad because you don't have to see them every day. Still, it can force you into more structure and more subjects than you think are healthy. Don't worry too much about the school board. Learn how to be diplomatic. Nod and smile and then go right on doing what you do.

The worst disaster by far is *you* refusing to trust yourself. You can suffocate yourself with guilt. If parents and teachers have not trusted you through a lot of your life, it is not your fault that you finally stopped trusting yourself too. It's their fault, but there's no point in revenge. Instead, work through it.

HELP

If anyone is still on your case with things you 'should' be doing, or nasty demonstrations of no trust, or if you find yourself tormented by guilt, school nightmares, or an inability to relax, get some help. Perhaps all you need is contact with other unschoolers. Maybe you need more intensive care, such as work with a counselor. On behalf of wise friends, I recommend co-counseling, although I am not myself a co-counselor.

And one relatively uncomplicated solution to some of these psychological difficulties is suggested by Judy Garvey and Jim Bergin, who have a 13-year-old son, in

GWS no. 76. An apprenticeship or job outside the home, they say, is the best way to make the transition to unschooling. Because it is a structured use of time out in the world, it combats any feeling of 'dropping out' or 'failure'.

'Hey, Miss Llewellyn, if it's so complicated and difficult for some people to heal from school, why are you so optimistic? How do you know I can recover?'

Partly because I've heard enough success stories. Partly because, like many adults, I have recovered too. It wasn't until I was in college, but my brain did finally boomerang back from the land of grades, SAT scores, tests, boredom, obedience and busywork. The revival, by the way, happened mainly through conversations with friends, and *not* because of any official college curriculum.

These stories and comments will help to illustrate the process more clearly. Sylvia Stralberg describes her vacation in GWS no. 80:

> Things finally got so bad this year in 11th grade that I said, 'That's it – I'm not going back to school any more', and I didn't. I had a few months of recuperation, which meant doing *whatever* I felt like doing, be it baking, reading, cutting out recipes or watching a movie. I had a lot of guilt feelings during that time about not being at school, but fortunately I have wonderful parents who reassured me that what I had done was OK.

Judy Garvey writes in GWS no. 76:

> Before children go to school in the first place, all their natural learning systems are intact. This is what we can see in families who have homeschooled their children from the very beginning. However, once children are in school for about three years, they are forced to shift over to a very unnatural system to survive the emphasis on memorization and the daily stress, rigidity and humiliation of classroom life ... Most children are very hurt and angry about what has happened to them and to their peers in school. As long as they stay in school

that anger must remain under control. When they come home, it all begins to come out. It may show up in extreme highs and lows, negative emotional outbursts, or long periods of apparent depression.

Kathleen Hatley writes in *GWS* no. 45:

A change that pleases me very much this year was to watch our son Steve (12), who spent four years in public [state] school, and who spent his first year of homeschooling asking for 'assignments', become a more self-motivated learner. He became interested in mechanical drawing when I gave him a beginning drafting set and he spends a lot of time designing cars and space ships. He has discovered science fiction and reads Asimov, Bradbury, Heinlein and others with great enjoyment (he has always read a lot, but despises the school-type reading programs where one must answer questions to prove comprehension). We both enrolled in the IBM Systems computer course at the state Vo-Tech school and he thoroughly enjoyed that – the perfect classroom situation, in my opinion, no tests, no grades, just people voluntarily coming to learn about something which they were interested in, from a helpful expert in the field. Since Steve's career goals tend toward the technical at this point, he works very hard at mathematics, and at his request we added the Key Curriculum algebra and geometry series ... He surprised me this year by informing me that he didn't want to take a summer break from his schoolwork!

Fifteen-year-old Maya Toccata, of British Columbia, Canada, says,

Most of my time is taken up by living. Which involves rock climbing, writing, reading, working at a hat store, researching massage, aromatherapy, shiatsu, reflexology, and doing the layout and editing of a teen section in a small homelearning newsletter.

I have been homeschooling for two and a half years now and it has been an interesting process. Now I feel comfortable with what I'm doing and feel I'm doing enough, but I didn't feel that way at first. I had a hard time persuading my parents to let me unschool. So when I started I was trying really hard to make it look like unschooling was working for me and that I was learning a lot, but I didn't really care about what I was trying to learn so I just sort of hung around all day. I felt like I was a big fake. I thought I wasn't learning anything, but now when I look back I see that I learned more about myself in those few months than I have in nine years of school, at school I was trying to ignore my true personality to be like everyone else.

12 | Getting a social Life

Whenever I mention my work on this book, hardly anyone says, 'But how would people learn anything without school?' Instead, they say, 'But how will they make friends?'

The question kills me. Teenagers make friends in spite of school, not because of it. There is only one reason schools can claim to enhance social growth: thanks to compulsory education, schools are full of people.

Well. A slice of birthday cake surpasses its beginnings in flour, sugar, milk, egg and vanilla extract. Likewise, a healthy social life goes far beyond mere contact.

A healthy social life requires much more than indifferent daily acquaintanceship with up to 300 people born the same year you were. It starts with a solid sense of self-esteem and self-awareness. It builds in time – time to spend with other people in worthwhile, happy activities where no one loses, no one is forced to participate, and where conversation and helping one another are not outlawed. In other words, school fights hard to keep your social life from happening, even though defensive schoolpeople preach loudly that school is important for socialization.

As for romance. Affection, intimacy and passion really are not encouraged to take root in a linoleum room smelling of chalk-dust. A mystery-relationship belongs out in the big mystery-world.

So. School is detrimental to friendship and other social joys, insists your author. But where does that leave you? To have a social life, you at least have to start with raw material – other human beings. Since most of the people near your age are shut up in school, you do face a challenge. Now, you are not alone in your aloneness – *most* of the social structures of our society have broken down. In the last decade of the 20th century, streets are seldom neighborhoods; family members rarely know each other well; adults' work environments require so much conformity that people cannot see who their colleagues are. Friendship and community do not happen automatically. But with a little effort, you *can* make them happen, just as adults do. Don't sit at home and mope, and don't be unimaginatively convinced that you need school to have friends. Instead create your own social structure.

CREATING A NEW AND BETTER SOCIAL STRUCTURE

When school is the structure of your life, you run into people all the time. When school is not the structure of your life, you can build a better social structure instead of inventing each day from scratch. This approach frees you from having to make a continual effort to spend time with people: if you always meet Josefina and Nazir to play music on Thursdays, then on Thursday you don't have to say to yourself, gosh I feel kind of like spending time with someone but I don't know quite whom, or what I feel like doing. Here are a few of the many possible strategies.

1 Set up regular, scheduled contact with friends. Start an important project with schooled or unschooled friends, and set regular times to work together two or three times per week. These projects could be anything – writing a book, cleaning up a beach, starting a health information

library, making a music video, rebuilding the engine of an old pickup.

2   If you prefer to work independently, you can still share space with friends. Your arrangement could be simple: schoolfriends coming to your house to do their homework while you do your academic work, unschooled friends bringing a novel and lounging on your bed. Or your arrangement could be more complex: a workshop or other definite space in one of your homes where each of you kept projects in progress and worked in the warmth of each others' company, with sunlight streaming through the windows and music in the background.

3   Start a business that puts you into frequent contact with people – like custom-painting skateboards or tutoring Spanish.

4   Join clubs or organizations for people with similar interests. There are infinite possibilities, especially in a city: university outdoor programs, performance guilds, sports teams, Amnesty International and other charities or political groups, drum circles, mountain search and rescue, city planning committees. There are important non-school organizations specifically for teenagers, too. Look into church youth groups, scouts, youth orchestras and other musical groups, teen hotlines and support groups.

5   Start your own club – to work on environmental issues, cook desserts, undertake 'projects' like those described in point 1 above, or whatever. Advertise your first meetings by putting up posters at or near a school, or by having friends post fliers, or by placing a classified ad in a school newspaper.

6   Get involved in regular work that provides contact with the kind of people you like to be around.

7   Take a class outside school – dance, martial arts, bicycle repair.

8 Start a weekly study circle to explore a subject you're interested in – Zen Buddhism, Shakespeare, the history of your region.

SOME THINGS THAT HAPPEN TO MANY UNSCHOOLERS

- They keep up their friendships with schoolfriends, doing the same kinds of things with them that they used to. Sometimes, they feel frustrated because their schoolfriends don't have as much free time as they do.
- They grow closer to their families and start liking their parents and siblings more than they used to.
- They have fewer acquaintances. They develop stronger, closer friendships. They appreciate not having to spend time with hordes of people they don't have a lot in common with.
- Their friends include adults and children as well as people their own age. They get over any former feelings that they can't talk with adults. Anthony J Hermans, 17, was out of school between the ages of 12 and 14, though he is now in a private school. He wrote to me that unschooling 'allows an individual to meet (and learn to deal with) a wide range of people rather than being largely restricted to his peer group ... Homeschooling can provide an incredible boost in self-reliance and self-esteem which all but eliminates peer pressure. I feel very little pressure from my peers, as do other homeschoolers with whom I have conversed.'
- Younger unschoolers – around 12 and 13 – often appreciate not having to deal with the pressure of having 'boyfriends' or 'girlfriends' just to fit in and be popular. Older teenagers frequently feel that most of their schooled peers are immature, inexperienced and un-interesting. They fall in love and make friends with

people slightly older than themselves. Their relationships and friendships are strong and honest. In general, unschooling allows teenagers to stay 'young' as long as they want, but also to 'grow up' as soon as they are ready.

- They exchange letters with unschoolers and other people around the world. Sometimes, they travel to meet these people.
- Their friends are mostly people who share their interests. When I asked about the greatest advantages of unschooling, 15-year-old Michael Severini said, 'I can spend more time with people who have the same interests as me.'
- They grow more secure and feel better about themselves as a result of leaving the social world of school, a world which is often cruel, judgmental and nosy. (One researcher has even 'proved' that homeschoolers have significantly higher self-esteem than school students.[14]) Suzanne Klemp, 15, comments, 'My confidence has grown immensely – I am not judged for reasons such as clothes, money, or my looks ... My social life is better than it ever was at school. I meet people at the YMCA [where she teaches ballet] and ballet class, and I have adult friends.'
- They do sometimes feel excluded from the bustling social activity at school. Most of them, however, feel that this social activity is shallow and unfulfilling. They don't *really* want it, but sometimes they do fantasize about it.

WHAT ELSE CAN YOU DO IF YOU FEEL LONELY AND ISOLATED?

1 Take your feelings seriously. Human contact is crucial. Don't try to tell yourself it's not important to have friends. If you want to be in love, don't tell yourself that's silly. It's not.

In fact, our social needs are more important and basic than our intellectual and creative needs. If you let your social life end when you quit school, pretty soon you won't care much about learning and exploring the world. You'll want to get right back to your locker, because Tatiana will be rummaging in her locker next to you. Psychologist Abraham Maslow pointed out that people have a hierarchy of needs. Each of us has to feel a sense of belonging, love, acceptance and recognition *before* we can set out to fulfill 'higher' needs such as intellectual achievement and complete self-fulfillment.

2 Don't romanticize your memory of school. School does provide contact with masses of people. It does not make friends for you, or even provide an environment that is good for making friends. Everyone who goes to school, and everyone who doesn't go to school, has times of overwhelming loneliness. Being in a crowd doesn't necessarily help.

3 Take responsibility for your own social life. Make an effort to stay in touch with former friends. If you aren't invited enough, do some inviting. Throw a party. If you're lonely, don't blame the universe, me or yourself. Instead, do something about it.

4 Go to school sometimes. Eat lunch there, be in the choir, be a teacher's aid, go to assemblies. *See* chapter 16 for ways this can be worked out. If it can't be worked out, who will catch you if you eat with your friends? I know of someone studying sociology at college who routinely eats in a school cafeteria just to watch people interact in their school ways. No one has ever noticed that she doesn't belong.

5 Get to know your family. Cultivate your siblings and parents as friends.

6 The best solution of all: *get your friends out of school!* Let the vision spread ...

13 | Adults in a New Light

Now that you don't have to *obey* teachers and principals and prefects, maybe you can start some healthy relationships with adults. These relationships can take all kinds of shapes. Adults can be your friends, companions, jogging partners and other 'equals'. Since you already know about friendships among equals, I see no point in explaining 'how to make adult friends'. If you spend time around adults – in chess clubs or during political campaigns or wherever – you will make adult friends. Thirteen-year-old Mylie Alrich pointed out to me that when you don't go to school, 'the line between kids and grownups is almost not there'.

It is also valuable, however, to have unequal relationships with adults. To reach your fullest potential, you need mentors, role models and teachers. That's not just because you're a 'kid'. Adults also need mentors, role models and teachers in order to reach their fullest potential. No one should be bossing you around or giving you unsolicited report cards, but these guides *can* help push and encourage you to do things you might not be brave, determined or skilled enough to do on your own.

TEACHERS (AND TUTORS)

Teachers explain their knowledge in a specific area. You may or may not admire them as people-in-general. You do need to admire their expertise in whatever they're teaching you, or else find a new teacher. Some teachers become more than teachers – mentors or role models or friends. But it is fine to have a teacher simply in order to learn a particular set of skills.

ROLE MODELS

These are people you admire from afar. You watch what they do and how they do it. You study them to see what you can learn from them. You can have role models in the career you hope to go into, or role models for life-in-general. By giving you a picture of what's possible, they help you to challenge yourself.

OTHER ADULT GUIDES

Adults play many other helpful roles also. They can be spiritual leaders like gurus or rabbis or priests, experts you can ask for occasional advice or information, counselors, advisors. Adults can be teachers in unusual senses of the word: Australian unschooler Alex Banks-Watson says, 'One of my favorite things to do is listen to adult conversations.' In ancient Greece, philosophers wandered through the streets and countryside with teenage boys, engaged in dialogues about truth and beauty. In a talk at my college, Barry Lopez spoke about the Eskimo people, who have no word for 'teacher' or 'wise person' but instead recognize people who play the role of *isumataq*. The *isumataq* do not teach or preach, but in their presence, wisdom is revealed. I mention these roles because they can help you to see and encourage nuances in your own relationships.

MENTORS

Mentors pay a lot of attention to you and give you long-term help, advice, guidance and support. Depending on their style, they might also give you a push when they think you're not challenging yourself enough. Eileen Trombly provides an example in *GWS* no. 18:

> Amy, 14, has had ballet lessons from an older woman in town and has developed a unique, warm relationship with her over the years. The woman is now in her 80s, still participates in dance, and has a very interesting past which she shares with Amy. The lesson is one-to-one so there is always much time for sharing and feeling relaxed in each other's company. The teacher was once a ballerina in the New York Ballet troupe, owned a theater with her husband who was in vaudeville, was daughter-in-law of a former Connecticut governor, and was acquainted with Anna Pavlova. She has much to offer in the way of experiences, and her polished yet friendly manner has served to influence Amy in a very positive way.

And 17-year-old Sarabeth Matilsky, of New Jersey, writes:

> It was the autumn of '95, and my mother and I were sitting at our dining-room table with the hateful grammar book in front of us. Sighing with frustration, I was trying to understand active and passive verbs and what makes an object 'definite'. These daily sessions were definitely not introducing me to the joys of the English language. Though we continued to work with the book for a while more, after a month or so of discouragement I wrote to Susannah Sheffer [editor of *GWS*]. I asked her if she had any ideas for me – books to read, stuff to do, anything besides that dreadful book. She wrote back with suggestions, and she also offered to give critiques on my writing if I wanted her to.
>
> So, for over a year now I have been sending her my essays and articles, and she has been sending me her comments and suggestions, and answers to questions. I have written more in the past year than I ever did before, and think that is partly

because I always have someone to show my work to. It's great to be able to do that, I discovered, because even if I never end up doing anything with an essay (like getting it published), I learn a lot in the process and I have an audience of at least one thoughtful person. She is always respectful, and in return I truly value her comments. I've been having so much fun writing to her, and now when people ask me how I study English, I can honestly tell them that I do it by 'correspondence'!

You don't *need* a mentor to have a nice life. Furthermore, not everyone who wants a mentor finds one. However, people who do have mentors say that the relationship helps them grow and succeed much more than they could on their own.

If you'd like to have a mentor, how can you find one? Patiently. Mentors are not as easy to find as adult friends, teachers, tutors and role models. You can't just advertise in the 'help wanted' section – anyone who thinks of himself as a ready-made mentor is quite certainly *not* one. Most probably, a mentorship will develop naturally out of other types of relationships.

If you have an intense interest in music and take piano lessons, over time you will grow closer to your teacher. Eventually, he may begin to take a more personal interest in you, and one day you realize you have a mentor. After you've been leading tours at the science museum for a few months, the director asks you into her office for a cup of tea. It turns out she knows all about stars, and when you tell her you have been learning to identify constellations, she invites you on her next telescope outing. Two months later, you realize she has become your mentor.

There is no quick formula to follow; like most important human relationships, each mentorship will develop uniquely and at its own pace. If you know someone whom you think would make a good mentor, you can certainly encourage the relationship in that direction. Tell them you admire their work. Show your appreciation for any time they spend with you. Ask for their advice. Watch for small ways to help them out. If they teach classes, sign up – and put focused energy into your work. If they enjoy the role you are quietly creating for them, they will soon start to take initiative for developing the relationship. If not, they'll back away. Be sensitive. Don't force.

If you don't yet know anyone you'd like to have as a mentor, get more involved in what you love. This way you can meet lots of adults – potential mentors. Take a pottery class, volunteer at the zoo, join a writers' group.

An ideal mentor is good at what she does, and other adults respect her. *Your* feelings toward her, however, are the most crucial. In her book *Professional Women and Their Mentors*, Nancy Collins writes, 'In selecting your mentor, you should try to choose someone for whom you feel admiration, affection, respect, trust, and even love in the broadest sense.'

Some of your former schoolteachers have excellent mentorship potential – so long as they have the time to develop an individual relationship with you. Also, of course, they must have some expertise. Forget teachers who are obsessed only with 'teaching' itself and not entranced with their subject. Avoid attaching yourself to someone who wants mainly to 'help you grow up' or some such slobbery vague condescending controlling rot.

Don't forget old people. With time on their hands and a lifetime of experiences behind them, they can make splendid mentors, enriching their own lives and yours.

Also, mentors need not be sugary touchy–feely types who always encourage you to do what you feel like doing and who tell you everything you do is wonderful. I often work best with very demanding people, like Pat, my flamenco teacher, who snapped, 'Again! Lift your chin! Bend your knees! Faster! Don't look at the floor!' But if you prefer the sugary touchy–feely type, that's fine too.

Encouragement, recognition and warmth may be exactly what you need.

Once you have a mentor, relinquish a little bit of control. Remember, you picked somebody you trusted, so now try the things they suggest. Take the risks they ask you to take. Let them push you on to your tightropes.

Finally, think about your end of the bargain. How can you return some of your mentor's generous energy? Offer to help by cleaning her house or typing her novel. Realize that you will never completely pay her back for her gifts, and that she won't ask you to, but that someday you can obliquely return the favor by sharing your own white-haired expertise with some wild teenager.

14 | Starting Out: A Sense of the Possibilities

A DIFFERENT KIND OF TIME

Don't be a factory. Do a few things well instead of everything poorly. Big undertakings – like starting a town orchestra or trying to find the ultimate physics theory – do take time. If you love your big undertakings, that time is never wasted.

A DIFFERENT KIND OF STRUCTURE

Don't assume that structure has to be *school*-style structure. Personally, I despise the idea of school-at-home and the kind of schoolish schedule that would entail. But you can build your own structure centered around whatever you like. For some unschoolers, structure consists of five or more hours of daily music practice. For others, it consists of a fully-fledged computer programming business, or nonstop reading, or tinkering all day long with electronics.

One valuable kind of structure is goal-setting. This is the sort of structure which serves your desires (I want to build a windmill so I will do this, that and the other thing) instead of your sense of guilt (I should study chemistry every day for 45 minutes). Obviously, you are going to learn lots by setting out to achieve your goals; in the windmill department that's going to include physics, carpentry, geography and probably history – for a start. If your goal is writing a book on unschooling, you're going to learn about the homeschooling movement, about the publishing industry, about wordprocessing, about library research, about efficient versus inefficient original research, about law libraries, about words and about fear – for a start. If your goal is to restore the neighborhood swamp to health, you'll learn about chemistry, biology, politics, economics, your own muscles and organizing people – for a start.

If you are completely confused as to how to start structuring your life, here's one way: do 'academic' studies for two hours each day – not necessarily lots of subjects, or the same ones every day. Do some kind of 'work' or project for four hours. In your leftover time, read, see friends, talk with your parents, make soup. Take Saturdays and Sundays off. Sounds arbitrary? It is. I made it up, although it is based on a loose sort of 'average' of the lives of a hundred unschoolers, most college bound. Once you try this schedule for a month, you will know how you want to change it.

Quite possibly, you may need a structured plan because your state or country laws require that you submit one. If so, read this whole book for ideas and then try two brainstorming techniques:

1 Make a list of the subjects you have to cover. For each, write down all the ways you can think of to 'study' them, and a list of related books you think you might like to read. Also ask your family and friends.
2 Make a list of your most important interests. Then look at each one and consider how academic subjects could be related to it.

Here are some comments and morsels of advice from unschoolers on their experiences with school-style structure and other kinds of structured and unstructured learning. In GWS no. 35 a brave mother writes about her teenagers:

'What do they do all day?' Why is it that I don't know? *Why is it that I don't care?* We don't keep journals or go on field trips or categorize the day's activities into subject areas. I can't stand the dead smell of all those fakey thought-up things.

Eleven-year-old Halee Shepler, of Caracas, Venezuela, writes:

> The way I do my schooling is by answering three questions each year:
>
> 1 What skill do I want to learn?
> 2 What question do I want to answer?
> 3 What big problem do I want to solve?
>
> Usually one thing leads to another. For example, one year I wanted to learn how to train my horse. This led to the big question: 'How do individuals and cultures change?' One day when my instructor and I were working with my horse, she asked another rider to jump him without my permission. When my horse refused the jump, the rider beat my horse. So I wanted to solve the problem of animal abuse. I started to search for resources. In *Horse Illustrated* I found an article about the Tellington Touch Equine Awareness Method. I wrote and I got information.
>
> This led to a new problem that I want to solve. Linda Tellington-Jones wrote about the work at the Paralympic Games. I told my friend who is blind and does jumping about the Paralympics and she was interested in entering the next competition, but there is no committee in Venezuela. I am helping her in this. So you see how one thing leads to another. I hope to be a TTEAM practitioner some day, after completing the two-year program for horses and companion animals, and work in therapeutic riding.

After Eva Owens left 'one of the so-called top public [state] high schools in the country' at the age of 15, she wrote in *GWS* no. 105:

> I am by nature very unorganized. I decided that, with homeschooling, I wanted to be somewhat organized to learn

what I wanted to learn. Also, when I wrote up my homeschooling plan, the school wanted me to set objectives that they could follow up on. So way back in September I set goals for myself for the year. By December I decided that I needed a little more guidance than that. So I sat down with Leslie [an adult friend], and with her assistance I set my goals for the coming month. Ah, but that was not enough for Eva, the procrastinator. Now in April I've become quite content with the routine of, after eating breakfast, writing down what I want to accomplish that day, with thought to my monthly goals. This has turned out to be best for me. At the end of the day I can see the results of my work and can see what I have not done. It's very clear cut that way.

Gwen Meehan, mother of 15-year-old Patrick, writes:

Last year was licking wounds and healing time. We both put much more emphasis on structured learning. We 'did history, English, algebra' and other 'school' things. It was fine and necessary for that time. Over the summer, however, I read all my back issues of *Growing Without Schooling* which highlighted homeschool information for older students. By the time I had finished, I realized the overwhelming consensus was: get off the formal education road entirely. Every parent and every child backed up the idea of simply letting the student direct his/her own education. My role would be 'facilitator'. I did not have to worry about 'teaching a curriculum', no matter how loose. This has been the proper direction for us. Patrick is developing wonderfully ...

Other parents wrote: 'The only books we regularly use are [for mathematics] books, because [mathematics] is easier to stick with if we use a specific book.' 'Throw away the textbooks, tests, and timesheets.'

Teenagers wrote as follows. 'We study reading, mathematics, English, spelling, social studies and science. We stuck close to [our] textbooks for our first two years. This was no different from being in school, and caused a lot of stress for all of us. It was also *boring*!' (The writer now uses textbooks only for mathematics.) 'If the school sends you a curriculum guide, ignore it. You'll learn a lot more going at your own pace.' 'Don't try to imitate school. Take areas you are interested in and learn from there. Find adults who know about subjects you are interested in and learn from them.' 'Don't schedule yourself too tightly. In school a lot of time is spent just moving from class to class, being counted, disciplined, organized. You don't need to structure everything. Be relaxed. Take time to talk. Take time to think. Do nothing sometimes. Ask questions. Don't force learning. Some days you're just not in the mood, other days you don't want to stop.'

DON'T SINK TO THE LEVEL OF SCHOOL

Dream the biggest dreams you can, and then follow them. Start a cultural exchange program for Japanese and American teenagers. Build a log cabin and furniture to go inside it. What you lack in skill and experience, you can make up for with time and patience. Don't rush.

REMEMBER YOUR ADOLESCENT POWER AND MAGIC

Don't spend all your time on mental stuff. It's not natural. You have your whole life to be academic. You have only seven years to wiggle and pray in a teenage body.

Life doesn't get worse, but it does get less intense. Things become less new and hormones stop raging. So honor and treasure your passion while it peaks. I'm not telling you to act on your every whim or to do stupid things like get pregnant when you're not ready to be. I am telling you to cling stubbornly to your spiritual yearnings, not to be talked into any imitation reality, to fall in love with people and, as Thoreau put it, to suck all the marrow out of life.

PART 3 | The Tailor-made Educational Extravaganza

15 | Your Tailor-made Intellectual Extravaganza

The next few chapters put access to academia in your lap. Before you ignore this advice, or – worse – before you approach it with determined despair because you 'should', please listen: intellectual fervor is for everyone. Maybe you don't think so, because when they made you do worksheets in history, biology or English, they stole from you the desire to investigate the past, marvel at caterpillars, or hear a good story. *Don't let them get away with it.*

Or maybe you don't think intellectual fervor is for you, because you think you know where your territory is, and it's anywhere – under the hood of a pickup, in the cosmetics section of a department store – except in academia. Wrong! The universe is your territory. You don't have to take a test to be allowed into the community of intellectuals. It doesn't matter whether you used to get A's or F's. If you read slowly or have a small vocabulary, you can read slowly and like it, and you can ask a person or a dictionary about words you don't know. If your father does nothing after work but drink beer and watch TV, that doesn't ban you from the poetry section of the library. If *you* do nothing after school but drink beer (or Dr Pepper) and watch TV, that doesn't ban you from the poetry section of the library.

HOW DOES IT WORK?

Getting educated in the big beautiful sense needn't ruin your day. If you devote two hours each night to reading and sometimes writing, conducting scientific experiments or tackling other mental exercises, you will certainly learn far more, and far better stuff, than you have been learning in school. Of course, you may wish to spend more time on 'educational' activities you love. But don't feel obliged. After all, you never spent a lot of time learning at school. As Micki and David Colfax (whose homeschooled sons went to Harvard University) point out in *Homeschooling for Excellence:*

> The child who attends school typically spends approximately 1,100 hours a year there, but only 20 percent of these – 220 – are spent, as the educators say, 'on task'. Nearly 900 hours, or 80 percent, are squandered on what are essentially organizational matters.[15]

ACADEMIA IN WHAT YOU LOVE

The next few chapters tell you how to study school subjects without school. They can help you both learn things you are already interested in and discover that you like more intellectual stuff than you ever thought you did. But at the same time, you can sweeten your life by giving your brain to the things that already have your heart. It's mostly a matter of realizing that there is no cement wall between the things we do and the things we learn. Rather than look for things to do that fit into a 'subject', look at the things you already like to do and think about where they might take you if you didn't stop them.

SOME UNSCHOOLED WAYS TO LEARN ANYTHING

Throughout the following chapters, you'll find heaps of specific suggestions for ways to learn without school. Chapter 16 lists resources you can find in your community. Here are a few activities that can enhance your learning in any subject but don't fit in the 'community' category.

* Create a small museum or display that relates to your interest – natural history, local art, archeology, skateboarding. At college I lived in a house with people interested in natural history. We kept a little museum in a back room full of a charming disarray of rocks, shells, fossils and dilapidated iridescent taxidermed birds. In other words, you don't have to be rich or famous or hired by the government to start your own museum.
* Write papers when you're really interested in a subject – one of the best ways to develop and clarify your knowledge and opinions. Writing can be a sharp tool that helps you reflect and draw conclusions on any experience or topic. You can write much more precisely than you can talk, because you have time to organize and think through complicated arguments and ideas. For inspiration, find academic journals in fields you like. If 'papers' and essays are too strenuous for you, write your thoughts about what you learn in an informal journal.
* Read academic journals, but only if you're ready to be patient. These journals (magazines) are written by and for specialists – they do not attempt to entertain the general public or to explain anything in easy language. Look in a college library, where you'll find magazines like *The Journal of Psychohistory*, *Sport and Exercise Psychology* and *Research in African Literatures*.
* Write letters to people and organizations, asking thoughtful questions big or small. Especially write letters to people you admire. Be extremely polite, but without

being self-deprecating. Enclose a self-addressed stamped envelope. If you write to people who aren't terribly famous your chances of a thoughtful response are better – not because famous people are heartless, but because they are already swamped with mail. Unschooler Chelsea Chapman writes in *GWS* no. 69:

I write to a former US Olympic Equestrian Team trainer who writes to help me with training and riding our horses. I started writing to her last fall when we were having trouble with the training of our Norwegian Fjord colt. I got her address out of a newsletter put out by the Norwegian Fjord Horse Registry and sent her a letter asking how she dealt with her Fjord horses. She mostly writes and tells me stuff about her horses and training methods and tack.

• If you have a computer, find software that can help you learn what you want to learn. It need not be expensive; you can download free software and inexpensive shareware from the Internet, or you could buy commercial programs together with friends or other homeschooling families.
• Form a study group to investigate a subject that interests you. Or consider hosting or joining a 'salon' – a regular discussion session with friends or acquaintances.

A LITTLE SERMON

Probably it's sad if you leave school and don't read any challenging books, but it's not the end of the world and certainly not enough reason to despise yourself. How many adults you know find two hours each week, let alone each night, to edify their souls through 'education'? OK, maybe some of them went to college and supposedly learned everything they ever needed to know there, but how much of that do they actually remember?

Everyone has their own clock. Though I got mostly As at school, I learned little. I forgot things soon after tests because most of the curriculum meant nothing to me. So much for informed citizenship. However, as my interests have broadened in the few years since I've been out of college, I've effortlessly amassed quantities of useful knowledge in widely varied subjects. In other words, I suffered from a poor education when I was a teenager, but this poor education did not prevent me from opening my eyes and getting on with things a few years later. If you don't read now, you can read when your hormones wane.

16 | Beyond 'Field Trips': Using Cultural Resources

In order to go about acquiring this tailor-made intellectual extravaganza thing that you will call an 'education' when talking to the school superintendent, you'll want to draw from a variety of cultural resources, including libraries, museums and other palaces of wisdom. If you live in a big city your largest trouble will be choosing the prettiest palaces from a kingdom full of them. If you live in a rural area or smaller town, your choices will be limited – you have more natural and agricultural resources instead. But no matter where you live, information abounds, especially if you have access to the worldwide electronic community called the Internet. Once you know some ropes, you can find whatever you need.

THE PUBLIC LIBRARY

This is the most valuable resource for most people's educations. We ought to have much less school and much more library. In a library, you can learn whatever you want, but no one will try to make you learn anything. You can find treasure in even a small library. With either a librarian's guidance or a small dose of courage, desire and knowledge, you can find *real* words: novels or poems that awaken your spirit, nonfiction that explains how to do anything – blow up a dam or build solar panels or make cream puffs or get a children's book published or choose a tennis racket or sew a seam or write a bill and find someone to help turn it into a law.

There are two ways to use the library: with an agenda and without an agenda. *I cannot over stress the importance of having no agenda*, at least occasionally. School makes you think of the library as a place to go when you want specific information about a specific subject. That's one thing the library is for, of course.

But the library is also a smörgåsbord of surprises. Sometimes, go to the library and walk into the shelves and see what's there. Forget the catalog, and don't try to think what subjects you might be interested in. You don't have to read any books you find, or even take them out, but pick them up and read their back covers and flip through a few. Also, check if your library has an oversize section (for large, tall books) that's where you'll find lavish art books, photographs of Balinese dancers, and such.

Using the library *with* an agenda takes a bit more skill. Unfortunately, if you're like most teenagers and many adults I've worked with, you don't know how to use the library, even if you think you do. You'll spend a lot of time there, so check out the territory thoroughly:

• Sign up for a tour, or ask for a map.
• Find out what your library has besides books: maybe CDs, videos, pamphlet files, career files, phone books, newspapers, bulletin boards, a local history section.
• Check out the magazines. They're more useful than books when you're looking into a subject that changes or develops rapidly, like political issues or fabric dyeing techniques.
• Don't be embarrassed to use the children's and young adult sections. Smart adults use them all the time.
• Use Interlibrary Loan to get books your library doesn't have. You'll have to fill out a form and probably pay a dollar or two.

• Also get to know local college and university libraries.

COURSES

Find out what courses are available in your community. Check: dance and martial arts studios, museums, art centers, community education listings, foreign language or culture centers, college and university catalogs, community colleges and as many other sources as you can think of.

LOCAL COLLEGES AND UNIVERSITIES

A college or university provides a continual array of lectures, concerts and workshops open to the public. Find out about these events by reading college newspapers or checking college bulletin boards. Many homeschoolers take courses at junior or community colleges.

LESSONS

Music teachers put up their cards in music shops. Sewing teachers put up their cards in fabric shops. Foreign language tutors put notices around college campuses. Also check the classified section of the paper.

TV AND RADIO

Relying on either too heavily will make you into a passive un-person, but do consider checking the TV guide and phoning your local radio station to ask them to send you a program guide.

MUSEUMS, ART CENTERS AND SCIENCE OR TECHNOLOGY CENTERS

These are more than exhibition halls, though when you're not in field-trip mode the exhibits themselves can blow your mind. These institutions also

- need volunteers
- have internship programs
- give demonstrations
- have classes, workshops and events which are open to the public
- have private libraries which they might let you use if they know you (maybe after you've volunteered for a while sorting dead butterflies into different trays)
- have staff who are experts in their fields

NOTICEBOARDS

Every community seems to have at least one place where people put up notices and fliers telling about events, lessons, used flutes for sale. Try natural foods stores, laundromats, cafés popular with college students or healthfood-eaters, and independent book shops. Also, when you want to get your own message or advertisement out, make a flier and stick it up.

SMALL, SPECIALIZED RETAIL STORES

These are a terrific place to start learning about a lot of things. The people who sell outdoor equipment, weaving supplies, garden tools, South American folk art, solar panels or ballet shoes often have considerable expertise in their fields. You can also learn a lot by walking through such shops and glancing through any magazines or books they sell. When a particular store owner helps you, return some goodwill by buying your supplies from him or her. Sometimes small shops have higher prices than huge chain stores, because they can't buy in bulk and have to pay higher prices for their goods in the first place. Just remember that when you spend your money, you vote for the kind of world you want to live in. Would you rather live in a world full of superstores or a world where Mike owns a friendly bike store down the street?

THE INTERNET

The magic of the Net has to do with its lack of hierarchy and with empowerment. Anyone – 9 or 90, working class or upper class, PhD or dropout – anyone with access to a modest computer and modem can both use the Net and express themselves on it. Anyone can use it both to learn directly from experts and to share their own expertise.

The magic of the Net also has to do with incredible generosity. Many, many people eagerly share their knowledge, whether it has to do with the Net itself or their other interests. For instance, on the Middle Eastern dance mailing list I subscribe to, many of the top national performers and seminar teachers cheerfully and unpompously answer the questions, often in great detail, of people who just took their first dance lesson last week. Yet the welcoming atmosphere also encourages less experienced dancers to add their perspectives.

If you're new to the Internet, you can find out everything you need by contacting a local service provider (look up 'Internet' in the telephone book yellow pages). Or you can sign on with one of the corporate giants such as America Online or Compuserve.

Don't feel you need the latest and greatest computer

gadgetry to take advantage of the Internet. An inexpensive computer will do; put your extra techno-budget toward the fastest modem you can afford. A good monitor is nice for viewing graphics on the Web, but you'll do OK with an older model. I've had the same computer for six years. It was an IBM-PC compatible 286 when I bought it; my brother helped me inexpensively upgrade it and add more memory and a fast modem, and it does a splendid job of bringing the Web-World to my screen.

Don't give up if you don't find something the first time you look. Realize that the Net is always changing. If you try something and it doesn't work, phrase your question another way. Search for the name or subject of what you want instead of its specific (maybe outdated) address.

And *don't worry*. If you don't have access to the Internet now, or if you're just plain not interested in it, *that's OK*. The information age will not leave you behind. One of the very best things about the Net is that as it develops, it gets increasingly easier to use, and shows every sign that it will continue to do so. When and if you do want to get wired, it will take you only a couple of afternoons to get used to it, and a few weeks to get truly proficient at navigating. If you decide at some point that you want to get involved at a more intense level – say, by designing elaborate Web sites or software – then *at that time* you can learn the skills you need, whether that is programming in a particular language (perhaps not yet invented as you read this) or some skill that we don't yet have a name for.

The computer manufacturers, magazines, software companies, Internet providers and the rest of the gigantic computer industry want you to be afraid that if you don't get on the Net yesterday, you'll be left behind. I want you to stand up to that fear. Ironically, you have not only your own brains to trust (and that's plenty), but also the Internet itself. Yes, every day it gets richer and more complex. But every day it also gets more intuitive, better organized and interconnected.

SCHOOL AS A CULTURAL RESOURCE

This book has said a lot of nasty things about school. Now it's going to say something nice. Schools have darkrooms, weight rooms, computers, microscopes, balance beams, libraries. They have choirs, bands, track teams, maybe even a Spanish class you like. Many enterprising homeschoolers have found ways to use the school resources they want without having to endure everything else. In some states homeschoolers explicitly have the right to participate in one or more elective classes or extra-curricular activities. In other states, and in the UK, there are no such formal privileges, but sometimes individual homeschoolers or families are nevertheless able to participate in the school activities of their choice.

Other homeschoolers decide to attend school part time, and convince local officials to cooperate. In *GWS* no. 33, Pennsylvanian Janet Williams describes her 13-year-old daughter Jenni's new schedule after previous years of pure homeschooling:

> Her schedule is as follows:
>
> Monday – 1st period Computers, then home
> Tuesday – 1st Industrial Arts, 4th Recess, 5th lunch, 6th Science, 7th Physical Education 8th Art
> Wednesday – 1st Speed Reading, 4th Recess, 5th lunch, 8th Chorus
> Thursday – 1st Spanish, 4th Recess, 5th Lunch, 6th Science, 7th Physical Education, 8th Bi-weekly clubs
> Friday – home all day
> Periods when she is not in a class, she works independently in the library or computer room.

Even if you are not officially enrolled at school, schoolpeople are likely to give you what they can, especially if you're nice. Fourteen-year-old Pat Meehan of Florida wrote to me, 'The schools here are very helpful. We

get a lot of our videotapes from the county teachers'
professional resource center through the school I would
attend if I were going to school. Everything is very cordial.
Some of the teachers are watching how we do because they
are thinking of homeschooling their own children.'

Another way to get access to the school things you want
is to skip the legalities and quietly go straight to the people
who have what you need. The choir director may just be
overjoyed to let you use a music practice room during
lunch. Can't hurt to ask.

AND DON'T FORGET

Zoos, ports, workplaces, the phone book, churches, city
governments, factories, arboretums and gardens, ethnic
festivals, hobbyists, parks and pools, clubs and
organizations, travel agencies.

17 | The Glorious Generalist

'What, Miss Llewellyn, is a glorious generalist?'

A generalist, in general, is someone who knows about a lot of things. But a glorious generalist must be distinguished from the heap of ordinary generalists.

The cheap flash generalist merely knows a lot of trivia. If he is especially flashy he can also recite amusing quotes by famous people. Nothing wrong with that, but the glorious generalist goes way beyond.

The almost-but-no-cigar generalist knows a lot about a lot of things. But it stops there.

If the glorious generalist has a lucky tricky verbal mind, he too can spew trivia and quotes. And pretty likely, the glorious generalist knows a lot about a lot of things, but not until he has been in business for a while.

The glorious generalist sees the world whole.

Because he sees the world whole, the glorious generalist can communicate thoroughly with people of every profession, religion or background. He can pick up any book or magazine and find in it a connection to his own interests. If he is an all-the-way-there glorious generalist, maybe he can do mystical/scientific things like read the meaning of the galaxies in a fistful of sand.

HOW YOU, YES *YOU*, CAN BECOME A GLORIOUS GENERALIST

Become a student and observer of a glorious generalist

First, you'll have to find one. (A lot of mothers, by the way, are closet GGs, though they probably haven't noticed.) You can check your candidate out to see if she meets some of the following criteria established by the nonexistent Criteria Board of the Universal Committee of Glorious Generalists. But if she fails the test, that doesn't rule her out. I hope you have some intuition, because you'll need it for this and later in life also.

1 Does the suspect take you seriously? If she knows you, does she ask you questions that go beyond mere politeness? The glorious generalist wants to learn from *you*.
2 Does she exhibit a wide range of interests? This sometimes shows up in a tattered, diverse library, or in scrapbooks or menageries or cluttered projects.
3 Are her friends a motley crew? Are they a mixture of young and old, this profession and that, three religions and five philosophies, hippies, yuppies and rednecks? (Not that the glorious generalist herself would describe them so slickly. She tends not to slap labels on people.)
4 Does she attend to the basic structure of her life – what she eats, how she cares for her body, how she treats her plants?
5 Is she unintimidated by specialists? Does she judge people on their capabilities rather than on their degrees? Is she brave enough to decorate her own house, raise her own kids, without worrying that she's not an 'expert'?
6 Have you ever heard her laugh and say, '*Every*thing is connected!'

Once you find this person, try to hang around and notice how she thinks, talks and finds things out.

Read the biography of a glorious generalist

Or read a book written by one. A few good ones: *A Pattern Language* by Christopher Alexander, *Laurel's Kitchen* by Laurel Robertson and *The Power of Myth* by Joseph Campbell with Bill Moyers. Often, the glorious generalist has written one or more books that make an ordinary subject seem wonderful and infinite, or a complicated subject seem understandable and fascinating. The glorious generalist can zoom up and down on the scale of broad to specialized knowledge. A good way to find out about glorious generalists' books is to perk up your ears when someone says, 'Well, it's a book about baking bread [or about political campaigns, or whatever] but it's really a book about life.'

Cultivate the habit of browsing

Make it a point of view and a way of life. If you deliberately sniff out the territory, you will have constant fun knowing new things, and every once in a while you will run into something unexpected that changes your perspective.

Browse in the realm of words: sometimes when you are in a library, just wander into the shelves and look at what's there. Look at the piles people have left sitting around on tables. Notice the variety of magazines, investigate a couple. Do the same in bookstores, preferably strange and atmospheric bookstores. Look to see what books friends have on their shelves. Ask which are their favorites. Take a mental bubble bath in the children's library. Flip through the telephone book yellow pages at home and the college brochures at the library. Read the newspaper now and then. Know what's on TV and radio, and tune in when the moon turns blue.

Browse in the material world: walk somewhere new

every few days. Go into a different store, take a different trail, look in the pet food or cookware section of the supermarket, swim in a different stretch of the river.

Ask big questions of people you meet

Find out what they do (even if they go to school – what else do they do?) and trust that they can explain their interests and work to you. See if you can grasp the essence, the ultimate point, of what they do. A few good questions you could ask are:

- What got you interested in what you do?
- What were the first steps you took to get involved?
- Why does your work matter? Where does it fit in the world?
- What questions are you asking in your work? (Or, what problems are you trying to solve?) How are you trying to answer or solve them?

Sometimes you will run into people who really can't explain for you what they do. Put on your suspicious hat. If it can't make human sense, does it make any sense? Some people in government bureaucracies don't seem to know any more where the ground is. That's the kind of out-of-touch mentality that's going to blow up the world, if anything is going to. The good (and strenuous) book to read on this subject is *Standing By Words* by Wendell Berry – very glorious.

Be ye not frenzied

(Teachers in school cannot easily be glorious generalists because they are frenzied. In this sense they are deplorable role models, although their frenzies are not their fault.) The idea is not to fill your mind up like a crowded refrigerator. The idea is to weave a prayer rug out of everything that comes your way.

Pay attention to the details of your own life

Such as what you eat, how you speak to your friends, how you walk down the street. The better you understand yourself, the better you understand everything else. You stand at the center of your prayer rug; you can't leave yourself out.

Let yourself cross boundaries

Be prepared, while you are reading Blake's poetry, to come up with a physics question you want answered. Entertain yourself with treats that stir it all up, like the artwork of M C Escher – as Stewart Brand describes it, 'Geometry set at its own throat via the images of dreams.'

Ultimately, education is about connecting with the universe, making our place in it. The more we connect, the bigger our lives and dreams. Through what we undertake to know and understand, we can be as immense as the Milky Way – glorious indeed.

18 | Unschooling Science and Technology

Science is one of the best reasons to quit school.

It took me a while to understand this. Several college admissions directors told me that their unschooled applicants had weak science backgrounds. Among the teenagers who wrote to me about their unschooled lives, a few said they felt as if they had skimped on science. Coming from an unscientific background myself, I felt as if I were encroaching on forbidden territory. In a bit of a panic, I thought about changing my title to *The Artistic or Literary Teenagers' Liberation Handbook*. Instead, I researched extra hard and called extra loudly on the expertise of my scientific friends – and I ended up believing that a mass unschooling movement could inject new life, responsibility and genius into the world of science.

There is no doubt that science presents special challenges to the unschooler. Laboratory equipment is expensive. Laboratory equipment is *intimidating*. This chapter tells you how to get past these difficulties, as well as how to make scientific use of the big wide world that schoolteenagers miss out on.

Why do unschooling and science go together? How should you approach science without school?

You have the whole universe, not just a gray room, for your laboratory. Use it.

School treats science all wrong. It usually allows no play and is afraid to ask you to do serious work. But real science is made out of play and very hard work, mixed together. It's a shame that we think of science as the most austere and forbidding of the disciplines, because the only way you can start right is to mess around. Tease your mind with inspiring books and trips to beaches and deserts. Make questions: why are clouds shaped like billows of ice cream? Why are all the trees in the park dying?

My brother noticed people in his first year at, Caltech, The California Institute of Technology, whose actual knowledge base was scanty – perhaps they hadn't yet studied calculus or much physics – but something had inspired them strongly enough that they craved the scientific tools with which to continue exploring their universe. This 'something' had varied – for one it was staring at the night galaxies, for another reading a rather poetic book called *The New Physics*. What they ended up holding in common was *questions* and *desire*, two of the best beginnings for anything.

Science also demands intense, serious work. Scientists have an immense responsibility to handle information carefully and honestly, in order to tell the truth about their subjects. Without a school schedule, you can take all the time you need for careful scientific investigations. You can wait for the right weather; you can observe the growth of molds for years instead of one lonely Friday in the lab.

Outside school you have the chance to get involved with real scientists and real scientific work. My friend Heather, a Watson scholarship finalist and final-year biology student at Reed college, suggests helping scientists with their research. Scientists always have more ideas than they have time to follow up, she says. A biologist, for example, might need someone to catch aquatic invertebrates, record information from climate gauges, check traps or collect water samples.

Phone up postgraduate students – who cannot afford to pay research assistants – and ask if you can help. Or put up fluorescent pink notes in university science buildings. If you live near a college without any postgraduate programs, approach final-year students, who will often have a labor-intensive project to complete, or professors. If you try this, expect to be inspected. Although you are offering free labor, you could completely ruin someone's research by being irresponsible with data. Heather says it's a good idea to do an inventory of your past before you start to contact anyone. List all the experience you have which shows that you can be precise and systematic. This could be descriptions of scientific work you've done on your own or at school. It could include recommendations from previous teachers. Work as a surveyor's assistant is the ideal background; certain kinds of cooking – making chocolates, for example – require precision too. So do woodworking and drafting. If you have little experience with anything of this nature, be ready to explain convincingly that you *know* you'll work carefully. If your scientist feels you aren't yet qualified, ask what you can do to become that way.

If you are artistic, or if the gray smelliness of most school science classrooms dismembers your enthusiasm, you can do lush colorful scientific sketching, particularly as a naturalist or geologist.

WHAT IS SCIENCE, ANYWAY?

Science is not, of course, planets and zygotes, but rather a careful, methodical process of looking at them. An important early task, in doing any kind of science, is knowing what this scientific method business entails. Unfortunately, school courses don't necessarily impart this understanding to you. They didn't to me. However, you can read about it in almost any science textbook, in the first chapter or thereabouts. Or in any encyclopedia article on 'science' or 'scientific method'.

Science has plenty of previously discovered 'facts' for us to learn, but the heart of science is the process of making questions and then searching for their answers. Please recognize, therefore, the difference between reading the results of others' experiments and conducting your own. Both are important, and some books are wonderfully inspiring, but actually to practice science, you must use the scientific method for yourself.

FINDING LAB EQUIPMENT

If you look hard enough, you will find the lab equipment you need. Here are some ways unschoolers find access to microscopes and other toys:

• By making arrangements with a teacher or school to come in and use equipment. This might work especially well if you offered to grade quizzes or wash beakers in return. Also, if you find an inspired teacher–scientist, you might end up with a mentor too
• By becoming involved as a volunteer, apprentice, student or indefinable presence at a museum or science center
• By using lab equipment at a parent's college or place of work
• By buying equipment. Aside from a good compound microscope, most isn't expensive, unless you want to have better facilities than schools do. If you want to buy, you can decide what to buy by making a list of necessary equipment for the labs in your textbooks
• By always mentioning your needs when you meet people. Gwen Meehan, mother of unschooler Patrick, wrote in *GWS* no. 73: 'I happened upon a marine biologist with a PhD. He has invited Pat to come and use his microscopes and ask questions any time he likes.'

DO YOU REALLY NEED LAB EQUIPMENT?

Maybe not as much as you think. Most lab experiments in high school textbooks don't demand much in the way of supplies. The most serious equipment any of them require is a compound microscope, Bunsen burner and triple beam balance. In the dozen or so textbooks I investigated, however, the majority of labs required little more than beakers, test tubes, crucibles, petri dishes, medicine droppers and graduated cylinders; and for physics a lab cart, recording timer, pulley, connecting wires and dry cell. You can even make do, in many cases, with substitutions. Use a candle instead of a Bunsen burner, any sort of scale rather than the triple beam balance, random plastic containers instead of official petri dishes, etc.

RESOURCES AND IDEAS

- Get a good science dictionary, like the Oxford University Press *Concise Science Dictionary*. A dictionary is useful if you want to do a lot in one science without studying the others. While you are reading about marine mammals and run into chemistry words, look them up fast here.
- Read popular books on science by inspiring writers like Stephen Jay Gould, Lewis Thomas, Aldo Leopold, Annie Dillard, Edward Abbey, Edwin Way Teale, Isaac Asimov, John McPhee, Stephen Hawking and Lynn Margulis.
- Check out children's experiment books from the library, like *The Chemistry of a Lemon* or *101 Physics Experiments for Children*. Without complicated equipment and procedures, there is nothing to distract you from the strange beauty of scientific reality.
- There's no law against using school or college textbooks and working through them at home; just don't let them rule your life.

- Put your scientific efforts to work for a local or national conservation organization – they all need volunteers from time to time to do things like count salamanders and monitor acid rain.
- Form a science co-op with other unschoolers or friends of any age. Buy equipment together, share ideas, discuss projects openly. Eventually, apply for grants together.
- Read scientific magazines.

A SCIENTIST WITHOUT SCHOOL

The *Christian Science Monitor* describes Vincent J Schaefer, one of the world's top atmospheric scientists, who left secondary school after two years. At 17, he and three other teenagers started their own small archaeology magazine. The New York State Department of Archaeology noticed it, and the state archaeologist invited Schaefer along on a month-long field trip.

In order to help his family earn money, he took an apprenticeship at General Electric. At GE, Schaefer found a mentor who encouraged him to conduct his own experiments in the laboratory. Eventually, without any college or university training, Schaefer discovered the first method of seeding clouds. In 1961, he founded the Atmospheric Sciences Research Center in New York. For the next 15 years, he directed it as the leading professor. The newspaper article passes along Schaefer's 'secret of success':

- Work on your own.
- Learn by doing.
- Seek out worthwhile people and make them your friends.
- Read books.
- Take advantage of every good opportunity to learn something.

- Remember that mature people enjoy helping young people who are trying to find themselves and realize their potential.

Shaefer insists that anyone with the desire could do what he has done. 'You have to have a sense of wonder,' he says, 'and be aware of everything that goes on. You have to develop what I call "intelligent eyes" – be intrigued with the world and everything in it.'[16]

UNSCHOOLERS DOING SCIENCE

Britt Barker followed her interests in wildlife and classical music instead of going to school. Starting at the age of 16, she traveled with naturalists in Canada, assisting them while they wrote a book on endangered species. She also received a grant to participate as a team member on an Earthwatch Institute expedition to study wolves in Italy.

After school age, Britt kept up her independent style rather than attending college. She again volunteered for Earthwatch, this time at the Bodega Bay Marine Lab in California. At 19, she was offered a three-month position for the autumn of 1987 at Point Reyes Bird Observatory in California, working with a biologist and four postgraduate students. Next, she spent six weeks tagging elephant seals for the Farallones National Wildlife Refuge near San Francisco. By that time she had been offered a winter job in Arizona monitoring bald eagles from land and air, using radio equipment.

Kathleen Hatley wrote in *GWS* no. 53 about her son Steve, 13.

> He developed a strong interest in freshwater fish. Aside from actually going fishing, which is his very favorite thing to do, he managed to read every available book in the library, including five volumes of a fish encyclopedia. He worked out a deal with

a friend who is a graduate student in fisheries, to supply him with worms and perch fillets for his specimens. In return, Steve received a large, fully equipped aquarium, in which to keep his own specimens. A highlight of the year was when he got to 'seine' a local river (drag the river with huge nets to bring up small fish to study) with the curator of the University Life Sciences Museum. Next week, he starts an apprenticeship with the ranger at a nearby lake (who happens to be one of the most knowledgeable naturalists around). He will be learning, among other things, how to manage a camping and fishing facility. This interest in fish led into many other areas, as a real interest always does – climate, pond and stream ecology, life cycles of insects, etc.

My older children continually reinforce my belief that when a child has an interest in something, they have a real need to plunge much deeper into the subject than a normal school curriculum ever allows ...

TECHNOLOGY AND COMPUTERS

People who work with technology are usually called 'engineers'. Another word for technology is 'inventions', scientific knowledge put to work for people – whether in the form of space shuttles, wind-powered laundromats or snowboards. Two terms which aren't mentioned often in school are 'appropriate technology', or 'sustainable technology', meaning the kind of machines and tools that use energy and other resources efficiently and wisely, things that run on solar, wind or human power (like bicycles), and stuff like sewage recycling plants and organic agricultural methods.

We need all the innovation we can get in this department. A lot of it will come from people who find out how civilizations did things before the industrial revolution, and then adapt these old-style methods and tools to fit 21st-century needs. You can be one of these people; *The*

Millennium Whole Earth Catalog (*see* Appendix) suggests excellent books and other resources. A living history farm or museum is also a good way to become intimate with such technology. Solar technology, by the way, is an area whose leaders have mostly learned all they know from independent experimentation and sharing ideas – not from college or other school programs.

Computers? Everyone already seems to know that there are a lot more self-taught 13-year-old computer whizzes than knowledgeable adult 'computer teachers', so I won't bother preaching that computers can be your unschooling friends. Barb Parshley writes in *GWS* no. 32:

> I am presently apprenticing in the most positive sense of the word, under someone who designs computers ... One day, as I expressed my regret to him for my not having gone to college for a degree in this field so I could work better for him, I asked him what his degree was in. He chuckled and said he didn't have one. Being sure he misunderstood my question, and also sure he must be progressing toward his doctorate, I restated my question. He said once again that he didn't have a degree, nor any school qualifications. In fact, he left at age 14. He is self taught, and is designing computers for companies both here and abroad.

And Noam Sturmwind, 14, of British Columbia, Canada, writes:

> As an adult I plan to be involved in the field of computers or electronics, or both. I have not chosen (up to this time) to take a computer course. I am entirely self taught; I have been unschooling since I was 7 years old.
>
> My learning has all been hands on; I use computer manuals and books from the library to assist in my learning, but also do much experimenting and playing around to find out what I want to know. I've taught myself several programming languages – C++, Visual Basic and HTML – as well as designing many small programs to do specific tasks. Some examples of the programs I've designed:

- A mathematics program where you can input any number and the program finds all the numbers that divide into your number evenly.
- Another program that finds all the prime numbers up to a number that you specify.
- A program that interfaces with an electronics project hooked up to the computer. It controls three LEDs (small bright coloured lights); the program gives you the option to flash them at a specified rate, allow them to turn on and off in sequence, or turn them on and off individually.
- Another program that interfaces with an electronics project: a door alarm. When someone opens my door, the computer greets them (out loud over the speakers) with whatever phrase I have entered.

Over the last few years, many people have asked me for computer consultations and help with problems, including my dad! I love the challenge of being able to sort out their problems and show them how to proceed.

I have been the Victoria Systems Operator for a British Columbia homeschooling bulletin board called 'WonderNet' for a few years now. This has involved setting up message areas and files, keeping the long distance gateway to the bulletin board in Vancouver operational, adding new users and upgrading the software.

For many years, my dad and I have done our own computer upgrading at home, adding and removing equipment or making changes to our existing hardware. We've taken our computers apart many times, and miraculously, they actually work when we're done!

Two possible volunteer positions I plan to create for myself involve working with computers. I plan to work in a used computer shop helping with repairs and problem solving; I've also thought about teaching computer skills to young children. This would allow me to combine my love of computers with my enjoyment of young children. I will also continue volunteering my time as a computer consultant to friends and family.

I am certainly the 'computer expert' in my family – when I

started exploring the world of computers, no one in my immediate family knew anything about them. Homeschooling has allowed me the freedom to immerse myself in my computer learning as much or as little as I choose to, at any given time. Because I have such tremendous flexibility and control over my own time, I have been free to pursue this passion while still following my other interests such as karate, swimming and skiing, indulging my love of nature, and avidly reading any and all books I get my hands on!

19 | Unschooling Mathematics

The world is colors and motion, feelings and thought ... and what does math have to do with it? Not much, if 'math' means being bored in high school, but in truth math is the one universal science. Mathematics is the study of pure pattern, and everything in the cosmos is a kind of pattern.

Rudy Rucker, *Mind Tools: The Five Levels of Mathematical Reality*

Most people leave school as failures at math, or at least feeling like failures.

Sheila Tobias, *Overcoming Math Anxiety*

BASIC SKILLS

These are extremely helpful if you plan on keeping track of your finances, car mileage or calories. Of course, you can use a calculator for most of life's necessities but, even so, it's best to understand what you're doing. If grade school didn't help you to develop your basic maths skills adequately, you can practice them on your own in a relaxed way.

NUMBERS PANIC

This often goes hand in hand with low mathematics skills. When we're scared of anything, it's impossible to learn. A book that can help you understand your fear and do something about it is *Conquering Math Anxiety* by Cynthia Arem. *GWS* magazine prints frequent suggestions which are honest, thoughtful and devoid of silly educational terminology.

HIGHER MATHS

That is to say, upper level algebra, geometry, trigonometry and calculus. Why bother? If you want to do anything scientific or understand theories about the nature of the universe, or if you want to design structures or invent technologies, numbers are a necessary tool. It is also the way a lot of people search for beauty. The *Encyclopedia Americana* says mathematics can 'woo and charm the intellect', and that 'the symbols can be employed neatly and suggestively, just as words are used in poetry'.

Does everyone need to learn this stuff? Certainly not. Too many of us school-educated people end up with more mathematics than we'll ever use in our lives, yet not enough to help us really *do* anything like build a bridge.

College? You may need mathematical skills to get in. How much depends on how selective the college is and how strong your other academic accomplishments.

TEXTBOOKS

Everyone seems to agree that the Saxons are the best in-depth textbooks. They make sense because they are easy to use without a teacher and because they are based on the principle of review. Instead of learning something and forgetting it, you do it again and again throughout the book until it becomes second nature, a living language rather than a forgotten vocabulary list. The texts include algebra, geometry, trigonometry and calculus. Saxon will provide a free diagnostic test to help you choose your level; there are homeschool packs which include the regular text plus an answer key; and experts also staff an invaluable phone 'helpline'. For a free catalog, write to Saxon Publishers, 1320 W Lindsey, Norman, OK 73069, USA, tel. 800-284-7019, www.saxonpub.com. Or try to borrow the books through a local school.

UNSTUDENTS

Amelia Acheson shows a bit of what's possible when she writes about her son in *GWS* no. 42:

> Alazel (16) loves math – he bought a set of accounting books from a local high school teacher and hurried through them. When he asked her for more, she was amazed at how far ahead of her classes he was. He also got a college supplementary text in trigonometry, and covered most of that between November and March. Then he set that aside and did no math for several months. About two weeks ago, he found his dad's analytic geometry book. It took him about three days to work through most of it, and demand a calculus course. In one and a half weeks, he has devoured about half of what college professors turn into a year's hard work. His dad has promised to coach him through physics when he gets integration under his belt ...

Andy, a 16-year old homeschooler in Germany, writes:

> Even though I have liked math since I was 7, I couldn't do much about it until we started unschooling when I was 11. Before that the class only went as quickly as the teacher let it, and the teacher wouldn't let us finish the math book in half a year. When we started unschooling I was able to work at my own pace and not the teacher's. Now, I am 16 and am in Trigonometry and Algebra III, having finished Algebra 1/2, Algebra I, Algebra II and Geometry by myself.

Dan Casner, 12, of Wisconsin, gives a behind-the-scenes view of what it's like to *use* mathematics for enjoyment and other real purposes, rather than simply learn it for some vague future:

Recently I made a probability chart of the odds of a given number coming up on several different combinations of dice. I thought it would be fun to do for its own sake and also thought it would be useful for a game that I like to play with friends. Prior to this, I had watched a PBS program on combinations, and tried several other models. The first one I did on the computer – I created a Pascal's triangle, though in this case it was shaped in a rectangle. (Pascal's triangle is a mathematical formula that my dad taught me.) I wrote some basic instructions and printed them out. After I tried to use it in real life, I realized it wasn't quite as good as I'd thought, and I did a little more research.

I did the next probability chart as a combination spreadsheet and wordprocessor program. And when I went at it still another time, my dad showed me how to use a computer program called Mathcad, which is designed to help math professors make diagrams for their presentations. But it is also useful for doing your own calculations. My latest chart showed probability for up to five dice, each with up to 30 sides.

I did a lot of the calculations in my head with help from my dad, during our walks with my dog. We talk a lot when we go on these walks and I do a lot of my thinking that way. And I get a chance to ask questions about science and electronics and chemistry and engineering and other things. On this particular excursion we worked out the mathematical formulas to use Pascal's triangle to calculate the probability of any given number coming up on the dice. I did the math, but he suggested some of the approaches and helped turn me round when I went the wrong way.

I've never in my life sat down to work on a maths textbook, although I have used books *about* mathematics. In this case, *Math Wizardry for Kids* by Kenda and Williams was useful as it showed Pascal's triangle.

20 | Unschooling the Social Sciences

My grandmother wanted me to have an education, so she kept me out of school.

Margaret Mead, anthropologist extraordinaire

This chapter describes ways to study 'social sciences' – history, geography, political science. These fields are related to each other, and they can grow more meaningful when they are allowed to merge a bit.

HISTORY

History is not merely what happened in the human past, although school doesn't usually point this out. It is rather the *study* of what happened in the past, and it is full of opinions, arguments and inconsistencies.

History goes far beyond dates, names of presidents and wars. Although that should be obvious, I mention it because it wasn't obvious to me until after I'd endured school and taken an enlightening college course. History asks all kinds of questions about relationships and patterns. What role did Christianity play in the rise of the medieval European medical profession? How did art influence peasant life in 18th-century Russia? Why are there wars? How did the experiences of early European explorers in America change European attitudes toward the natural world? How has the etiquette of warfare in Japan changed over the centuries? Where did compulsory schooling come from?

Understand the difference between primary and secondary sources: a primary source is a document (or sometimes a painting) produced by someone at the scene of the crime. A letter home from a soldier in the American Civil War is a primary source. A secondary source is a historian's interpretation of a variety of primary sources, like a textbook about the Civil War.

Since history is based mainly on written documents, it usually looks back only as far as a culture's written heritage goes. Archaeology – a branch of anthropology – looks further into the past, since its clues are found more often in physical objects than in words.

Here are some ways to explore history.

Historical novels

Some people think of historical fiction as a skewed, subjective view of the past. They're right, of course. But the same is true of any other source, primary or secondary. Historical novels can give you a greater feel for a time period than textbooks can. Usually, their authors are historians in their own right who do extensive research – reading all those textbooks and primary sources and visiting the setting of their work. Their novels often include notes in the front or back that tell about their research and other background information. Before you read a historical novel, you can increase your understanding of it by reading a brief description of the time and area in a good encyclopedia or historical atlas. Some good authors to check out are James Michener, Mary Renault, James Fenimore Cooper and Willa Cather.

Movies can be historical fiction too

Just don't be brainwashed. Recognize that any movie has an editorial perspective, no matter how objective it seems. As with historical novels, you can make more sense out of what you see by first checking an encyclopedia or historical atlas. A little background knowledge on the *Ballets Russes*, for instance, makes the movie *Nijinski* far more interesting.

Living history

Living history projects are one more proof that learning-in-the-world is far thicker and richer than learning-in-school. All over the planet, you can join groups of people who make a hobby, an education or a vocation out of re-creating a particular period of history, in lifestyle, costume, language and skills. You can find enclaves of medieval enthusiasts who joust in authentically crafted suits of armor, embroider stunning 14th-century-style dresses and teach each other to play music on ancient instruments. Other people re-create the battles of the English Civil War. Some living history projects revolve around farms.

More history activities

- Make a timeline. It could be general, or specific – the history of team sports, the Protestant church, anything.
- Visit places near you where the past is visible – sometimes this means an official historical monument, perhaps a restored house, even a cousin's attic, or possibly a rusty ghost town. Often these places reek of tourism; you may need to spend several hours just sitting, slowly conjuring up images of what happened

there, letting the tourists fade, almost slipping into a trance. It also helps to visit historical places when few people are present – at dawn, on Monday mornings, maybe even if you're lucky when a museum is closed to the general public. Remember, you are not on a school field trip. Don't be in field-trip mentality. Stay as long as you like. Be quiet and dream into the scented past.

- Record oral histories.
- Your own family history would surely love to be investigated and written down by you. In turn, researching such personalized history can make general history more meaningful. In GWS no. 36, Virginia Schewe writes about her 14- and 13-year-old boys as well as her 9-year-old daughter:

Quite by accident this summer, I opened the doors to genealogy and suddenly history became very interesting to the youngsters. After we discovered that a great-grandpa had been in the army during the Civil War, did a little research in the service records, traced his path, and read about the battles he had taken part in, the Civil War wasn't just some old dumb scrap any more ...

- Combine history with something else you love. If you like cars, get involved with the local antique car collectors' clubs. Or collect old jewelry, knives, books, tools, horse tack, gramophones, whatever. You can do this for free by keeping a scrapbook collection instead, cutting out pictures of such things in magazines and labeling them with notes.
- If you become a serious collector, open a small museum. It need not compete with the Smithsonian. House it in a spare room or even in a corner of your bedroom. You could open it to the public occasionally or only to friends and fellow enthusiasts.

GEOGRAPHY

The drumbeats we listen to, the earrings we wear, the fruit we eat – it all reflects the richness of a thousand cultures' traditions and talents. Geography is one of the most fun and lavish subjects you can immerse yourself in, especially when you are out beyond the limits of school.

Resources and activities

• Read *National Geographic* magazine.
• Watch movies set in cultures different from yours, fiction and nonfiction. Outstanding examples include *The Emerald Forest, Salaam Bombay, The Milagro Beanfield War, The Gods Must Be Crazy, Local Hero, El Norte, Wedding in Galilee.*
• Keep a scrapbook. Focus on pictures of worldwide dwellings, farming practices, celebrations, whatever. Those cheap *National Geographic* back issues come in handy.
• Find out what music from other cultures you like. Most libraries have some. Also check the 'world', 'worldbeat' or ethnic sections of music stores. Notice that a lot of your favorite music probably has strong ethnic influences. Peter Gabriel, for example, has been especially innovative in weaving global sounds into his work. If you are a musician, enrich your work by soaking up some faraway sounds.
• Learn to cook and eat the foods of a new culture.
• Put a map of the world or your state up on the wall. Look at it.
• Throw a party, combining several elements of a culture that interests you. You could re-create an entire traditional celebration, such as a Russian New Year's

festival, complete with an ice slide, costume workshop and authentic games. Or you could simply serve the right food and play the appropriate funky music.

- Go international folkdancing. You'll not only whip your feet through incredibly complex patterns, but also learn about geography, international music and costume.
- Have a pen pal. Fourteen-year-old Dawn Smith of Alberta, Canada, writes:

All my free time has been eaten up by a fast-growing hobby: pen-palling. My life has started to revolve around the mail, not the TV. Currently I have 77 pen pals from all over the planet. Probably half are inside Canada, the other half live anywhere from Berlin, Germany, to Bangkok, Thailand. I am happiest when I am crouched over my desk describing to Daphne what snow looks like because snow doesn't fall in Athens, Greece.

On my bookshelf, underneath Shakespeare and math texts, are two huge binders. These binders are my pride and joy, for they contain all the letters I have ever received. Along with a lot of letters there are numerous pictures, postcards and stickers. People naturally like to tell about their country and homes. Some are shy, but before long they are describing birds outside their window and the type of music that is played at the local dances.

Writing letters has let me out into the world. I am starting to realize that people everywhere (not just teenagers) are the same. My friend in South Africa likes the same music group as me! Having pen pals has made me more aware of the news. Peace talks and earthquakes seem a lot more real (or dangerous) when you know someone personally who might be affected.

Local geography: bioregionalism

This means living *where* you live. Bioregionalism means knowing and caring about the landscape and the people near you. It means cultivating the perspective that where you live is the most beautiful place on earth, even while you realize that every other place is also the most beautiful place on earth – for other people. If anything saves this planet, it will be people who love where they are – ceasing to live in abstract fantasies, plugging in and talking to their neighbors, noticing the first tree buds in spring, climbing the nearest hill to get a look at the contours of the land, going out dancing to local bands instead of being seduced only by the faraway stuff on TV, reading poetry by local authors, munching cherries from your neighbor's garden instead of mass-produced snacks.

A bioregionalist perspective will influence everything you do, from eating to reading to making friends to deciding whether and where to go to college. In your library, look up books on various aspects of your particular area – its history, the lifestyles and cultures of people who lived there first, its geological background and agricultural products. More importantly, go for walks in your neighborhood, eat in a café that is not a McDonald's or some other international chain, bicycle around the outskirts of town, get to know the pigeons or the homeless people in the park.

POLITICAL SCIENCE

When I first wrote this section, it was January 1991 and the US had just gone to war against Iraq. The world felt dark and small. If the worst continued, I thought, some of my readers would be sent to fight. In a letter to a former student, I wrote:

> If teenagers had more say in the world, the world would be a much cleaner, more peaceful place. The people who wage war and destruction have so little to lose, it seems ... they're no longer young, they won't be around to see garbage dumps and nuclear waste blot out the face of the earth, they're not the

ones who have to meet the 'enemy' face to face and shoot, they spend far more time with their documents and diplomats than with their grandchildren. It seems tragic and unthinkable that you are so alienated from the actions of your government.

Later, as I finished the first edition of this book, it was March 1991. The war was over; a cherry tree blossomed outside my window. We all breathed more easily, though across the world a country was in ruins. My sense of urgency had diminished, but the political structure of the world had not changed or improved. It *still* seems tragic and unthinkable that you are so alienated from the actions of your government.

How can you begin to make sense of it? I suggest getting *informed* and getting *involved*.

Get informed

Share the thoughts of the world's greatest political philosophers, and build your own 21st-century thoughts on top of their wisdom. Stay in touch with current events and you are better able to decide what changes need to be made in the world. Knowledge is power.

Political theory

Read the works which have most influenced Western political systems, like those by Plato, Aristotle, Thomas Hobbes, John Locke, John Stuart Mill, etc. Be sure to read Henry David Thoreau's *On the Duty of Civil Disobedience*. And read the US Declaration of Independence and the US Constitution, or the primary political documents of your country. Be aware of new political theories and models which often arise from the peace movement, the women's movement and new religious traditions.

Current events

Read a local paper once a week or more. Pay special attention to local news and politics, because locally your voice can easily make a difference. Read the editorial page especially, to find out how your community feels about things, and to clarify your own opinions. For national and world news, read the major daily newspapers. Your library probably subscribes.

National, college, 'alternative', 'pirate' and state-funded radio stations have excellent news programs and thoughtful in-depth interviews and commentaries.

Get involved

Build a bridge between you and what happens in the world. Go out in the streets with a sign or a flag, play your guitar at a rally, perform political street theater or organize a vigil. Write letters or e-mail politicians, distribute leaflets for political campaigns, knock on doors to ask for Greenpeace donations or help other people register to vote – though you yourself can't yet vote. Work to get a city, regional or national bill passed. March on the capital. Plugging yourself in will empower you and give you an unbeatable education.

Don't try to do tough political work on your own. Surround yourself with support, both practical and emotional. At times, all your efforts will seem a failure. Don't give up – your role is small but essential. Drop by drop, water makes an ocean.

21 | Unschooling Literature and Writing

The best English teacher in the world would hardly say a word, especially to the whole class at once. She would stay out of your way, let you read all you wanted and not try to organize any cute conversation about the motivations of the characters or the relationship between the setting and the theme. She would not keep you from writing by 'making' you write. She would sit peacefully at her desk, reading *Pride and Prejudice*. If you went to her, she would put her book down, smile and consider your questions.

Unfortunately, if this teacher ever existed, she has surely been fired by now, because every time the principal went in to check on her, she was not busy asking you the difference between metaphor and simile. She was violating the first law of teaching, which is 'Thou shalt be busy'.

Fortunately, since you are out of school, her nasty luck need not distress you. Instead, you can go and sit under the apple tree with your literary treasures. If you want conversation about setting and theme, or more intricate matters, you can go find it in the company of other people who want it too.

LITERATURE

Literature is words telling us our lives. Our lives are funny, profound and tangled. So are the good stories about them. The study of literature happens in two ways. The first and most wonderful way is simple – reading something because you like it. If you don't read for enjoyment, you lose. The second way, which is also wonderful as long as it stays honest, is literary criticism. That's when you first read something and then talk (or write) about it. Unfortunately, dull and insensitive approaches to criticism ruin a lot of people's love of reading, let alone their potential enjoyment of criticism. Too many college English students end up hating their former favorite books, after nailing them into caskets made of words like 'denouement', 'flat character' and 'narrative voice'.

Sometimes literary criticism seems utterly ridiculous, a way to make insecure English professors feel as scientific as scientists, even though they're not and shouldn't be. At its best, however, criticism can deepen your relationship with literature, enabling you to be twice as moved.

Criticism, by the way, does not mean saying *bad* things about literature. It means saying analytical, thoughtful things about literature, after asking such questions as: What does Shakespeare's use of the word 'nature' reveal about the relationships among Lear and his daughters? Can a feminist appreciate Edward Abbey? What effect does the concept of royalty have on Hamlet's fate? What is implied by the differences in Mrs and Mr Ramsey's language in *To the Lighthouse*?

Some people – could be you – can love this. Others can only laugh or run. There is no shame in feeling either way. It *is* a shame to turn against reading stories just because you don't like to dissect them publicly afterwards. It is a worse shame to perform literary criticism if you can't also simply enjoy reading for the fun of it.

Do you *need* to analyze the books you read? No, no, no, a thousand nos! You don't need calculus to use long division and basic algebra, or to get along marvelously in the world.

And neither do you need to get into deep criticism in order to love and be changed by great books.

Exactly which one of the 2,472,003 books should you read?

Nobody except a vampire has the time to read all the great stuff. That's good news for you, since it means your answer to the question 'What have you been reading?' is potentially as good as anyone else's.

Of course, there are a lot of books that count as classics, and a lot more that don't. What counts? Why is *Sweet Valley High* out and *Romeo and Juliet* in? No one quite agrees, but we have several generally accepted definitions: good literature is made up of written works that have endured the test of time and offer something of value to our present culture. It is made up of stories that take us beyond mere entertainment, raising questions about the way we live and die. Ezra Pound wrote, 'A classic is classic not because it conforms to certain structural rules, or fits certain definitions (of which its author had quite probably never heard). It is classic because of a certain eternal and irrepressible freshness.'

Why bother to read the stuff? Mainly for enjoyment, as I said already. To be lifted out of yourself, to fly, to cry. To broaden your perspective and to learn about human nature. We can look to literature when we face a dilemma or crisis, because literary works show different ways of handling all our situations – birth, falling in love, losing love, failure, success, betrayal, loneliness, watching parents age and die, wanting money, getting money, hating money, losing money, enduring war, facing death.

Resources for readers

Find a bibliography that is appropriate for you. A bibliography is an annotated list of books, and it helps when you're confused and lost in the literary universe. You've heard of Shakespeare, of course, but then you've also probably heard of Danielle Steele. Why should you read Shakespeare? And how do you know what else you should read if you don't have an English teacher? (Once you've been out of school a while, you will not feel insecure without teachers. At first you might. Therefore, the bibliography.) Your library may have a short bibliography printed up. A couple of book-length bibliographies I like are Clifton A Fadiman's *The Lifetime Reading Plan* and Erica Bauermeister's *Five Hundred Great Books by Women*.

Get a good anthology, too. An anthology is a collection of literature – a lot of stuff in one book. I highly recommend the various Norton Anthologies, such as *The Norton Introduction to Literature*, *The Norton Anthology of American Literature* or *The Norton Anthology of English Literature*.

Resources for critics

- *A Glossary of Literary Terms* by M H Abrams. Required in many college English classes.
- Hit the scholarly journals. Read a few to get an idea of whether you want to major in English or another literary field in college – the dense difficult papers in them are just the type of thing you'll be writing, again and again, in any English department. If you do like these journals, read them and become a precocious expert. Write your own criticism in the same vein. Eventually, send in an essay and see if they'll publish it.

YOU, THE WRITER

Basic writing skills

We learn by example. Therefore, the best writing teacher for most people is lots of reading.

Common sense, too, will take you a very long way. I've had several students who spoke articulately but panicked and fell apart when they had to write, because school had coached them to believe writing was difficult and mysterious. Together we found that all they needed to do was slow down and imagine themselves talking, and then write what they heard themselves saying in their heads. Simple? Yes. Silly? No. School doesn't often advocate common sense solutions, because if everybody trusted their common sense, they'd stop feeling they needed school 'professionals' to learn.

Be sure not to expect anything to come out perfectly the first time. At first, brainstorm, jot down your thoughts and just spill everything out freely. Don't bother about spelling, perfect word choices, punctuation, etc. You can organize and reword things the second time round. On the third pass, you can fine tune it, use a thesaurus, get rid of passive voices, check spelling, worry about commas. Writing is a *process*; for almost everyone, it requires several steps. If you try to get it all right in one step, you'll set yourself up for failure.

The basic idea is that you can't both create and censor at the same time. So first you write and create, then you censor and structure and limit. Three excellent books on learning to write expressively through this process are Gabrielle Rico's *Writing the Natural Way*, and Natalie Goldberg's *Wild Mind* and *Writing Down the Bones*.

If writing skills – especially punctuation, usage, mechanics, etc – don't come naturally, and even if they do, arm yourself with Strunk and White's classic, *The Elements of Style*.

Beyond basics: developing literary talent

Of course, to be a writer, all you really have to do is write. Frills like writers' conferences are unnecessary. And if you *don't* write, no amount of writing instruction will pull a novel out of your navel. Once you are actually writing, however, outside stuff can help.

- Apprentice yourself to a great writer by studying her work carefully. Some techniques: copy passages of her writing into a notebook (to help yourself understand her style). Try writing in her style. Read her best works again and again. Memorize parts of her works. Read her biographies, letters, anything you can find that tells *how* she wrote. Eventually, try the same process with a different writer.
- Start or join a writers' guild or support group. C S Lewis, J R R Tolkien and other friends met to share and discuss their writing in a group they called The Inklings.
- Take a course in writing – *if* you trust the teacher. It only makes sense to be taught by real writers. What right most secondary school English teachers (like yours truly) have to pretend to teach 'creative writing' is beyond me. Teachers need not be *professional* writers so long as they are willing to share their work and you think it is good. A lot of writers do teach, particularly in occasional college courses. If you don't find a writer–teacher, skip it.
- See your writing as a way to make a difference in the world – join Amnesty International and write letters on behalf of tortured prisoners, write your members of parliament or congress thoughtful letters about injustices that steal your sleep, write to the utility companies outlining your ideas about ways they could encourage energy conservation.
- Produce your own magazine or newspaper – one way to get your writing published as often as you like. Craig

Conley, a 15-year-old former homeschooler attending Louisiana State University, wrote about his newspaper in *GWS* no. 30:

I first got interested in writing newspapers five years ago when I was present at the collapse of a historic old hotel in Joplin, Missouri. I wrote an article about the history of the hotel and how it collapsed, trapping four men under the rubble. I added other articles about what my family was doing, and what was going on in town. Soon I had a whole newspaper ... Now my paper is read by 40 families, in 15 different states. It is called *Craig's Quarterly* and each issue ranges from 12 to 30 pages. It contains book reviews, news articles, artwork and stories. Subscribers send in articles they have written ... Reporting on activities ... is good training for life. It makes me more observant and analytical. I try to look at people I know and new people I meet as possible subjects for an interview and sometimes this leads me to ask questions I might never ask otherwise. The most fascinating people are really in your own backyard ...

22 | Unschooling Foreign Languages

The study of a foreign language is not really a discipline of the same intensity as the study of molecules or epic poems until you are far past fluency. As a beginner, you are not studying the language from an academic perspective; you are merely trying to speak and understand it, to use it as a tool. But as you learn, you may wish to flirt with interesting academic questions, like: how does a language reveal or shape the culture it belongs to? For instance, in Russian, the verb 'to get married' is different for men and women. For women, the term literally translates, 'to go behind a man'. In Cantonese, the symbol for 'angry' breaks down into symbols for two men and a woman. Why study a language?

1 In order to be able to communicate when you travel.
2 In order to read (for example, science in German or Russian, literature in Greek or French or Japanese).
3 Because you like words.
4 To get into a selective college.

HOW WE LEARN LANGUAGES

There may be a lot of mystery about how we learn languages, but we don't necessarily need to solve this mystery any more than we need to know why we like chocolate. By thinking for a few minutes about how children learn to talk, you will understand all you really need to know about learning a new language.

Any natural language learning starts with lots and lots of listening. Before most people can actually learn a language they need to hear it constantly for days or months. If you decide to start by working with a textbook, fine, but at the same time expose yourself to the sound of the language, through foreign movies, subway rides, college language clubs, whatever. That's the way babies do it, and they're the experts. Don't worry that you can't understand what you hear. Don't try too hard. Relax. Don't worry, be happy.

LANGUAGE FOR TRAVEL

If travel is your reason for learning, you don't need to learn until you actually arrive in a new country – if you have plenty of time, that is. Certainly the most exciting and vivid way to learn a language is to use it because you need it. If you like this idea, you can try several approaches:

- Find out about language schools in the country you will visit and plan to enroll as soon as you arrive. Often these schools will arrange for you to live with a family, if you wish. You can find out about trustworthy schools by checking travel guides in the library. Some areas are famous for their language schools. For instance, many people begin a journey through Latin America by spending a month in one of the many Spanish schools in Antigua, Guatemala.
- Learn how the basic sentence structure works and how verbs are conjugated. Memorize a few key phrases like 'thank you' and 'Where's the bathroom?' (This should take a few hours, using a book, tutor, tape course and/or video cassette.) Then take a dictionary with you and go. Panic on the plane and do some more last-minute studying. Make a complete idiot of yourself for a while.

Don't hang around with other English-speaking people. From personal experience, I highly recommend this method. In Third World countries, it's cheap. It's fun. It's life. It works.

• Spend a year or more learning a language through books or other resources. Once you feel comfortable with your skills, plan a short trip. This method demands self-discipline, and is definitely less romantic and effective than the previous two ways. But hey, it's safe. Your school board will approve.

• Enroll in a foreign exchange program. The obvious trouble is that you may have to go to school, which won't be any more fun, after the first few weeks, than school at home. But you can always try a *summer* program so you don't have to go to school.

LANGUAGE FOR OTHER USES

If you decide to learn a language for college, 'the future', or another abstract reason, choose carefully. This can be one of the more important choices you make in life since it can strongly influence what you are capable of doing, where you travel and what you can read. Consider the following factors: Are there countries you eventually hope to visit? What languages are most widely used? What are your interests and possible future plans? What languages are easiest? Do you want to learn the language of your ancestors? Will you need to read in a specific language? What cultures fascinate you?

RESOURCES

Don't rely only on books, tapes or other programs to learn a language. Removed from actual human communication, it's no fun and a little bit insane. But in combination with a native tutor or a foreign friend, programs can help you organize and practice your learning. In bookstores and music stores, you can find a variety of cassette programs that help you to learn a language through listening and repetition. Educational television has programs like *España Viva*. General and college bookstores also have various texts for learning languages. You might check to see what books local colleges are using and then look for a used copy.

ACTIVITIES

- Find out if your city has a foreign language center. Some of these centers not only offer classes, but also host regular lunches where people – both fluent and stumbling – talk informally.
- Find out when a local college or university has language tables. This means that during lunch or dinner in the cafeteria people who want to speak Japanese (or whatever) sit together and try to make sense.
- Go to foreign films, with or without subtitles. Better still, borrow a foreign video and watch it many times.
- Host a foreign exchange student – homeschooling families *can* do this, though the exchange student will go to school. If it seems a bit odd to live with a student when you are not one, try to set up an unschooling exchange by writing to *GWS*. Another possibility is to house a foreign college student. Contact the foreign student support services at local colleges to see if they can help with arrangements. Danielle Metzler, of Connecticut, writes in *GWS* no. 106:

I found learning Japanese without a teacher or textbook to be both challenging and enjoyable. The key was having the right attitude. This included realizing that learning is sometimes hard work. However, doing it for yourself is fun, is much easier and has a more lasting effect. I also looked for *every* opportunity to use what I was learning. My family hosted at least six Japanese exchange students over the course of 18 months. Between their visits I reviewed what I had learned and took in some more information from my CD ROM program and my grammar book ...

The exchange student program provided a sheet of survival phrases with a pronunciation guide. This sheet was not enough, so one of the first things we did was buy a very good English–Japanese dictionary. I made sure it was small enough to carry around wherever we went. It had phrases and a pronunciation guide. We also bought a book on Hiragana, the primary Japanese alphabet. Even though there is also another alphabet and pictogram system with thousands of characters, I was still thrilled to be able to recognize a few words now and then.

The one thing that helped me the most was talking with someone who is Japanese. It is essential to understand how words are pronounced right away. This helps eliminate a lot of confusion ...

I think homeschoolers benefit by sharing what they have learned, so I did just that. I prepared a three-hour practical presentation of the Japanese language and culture for homeschoolers in my support group. Some of the things I shared with them were origami, basic Hiragana, introduction to conversational Japanese, some of the gifts we received from our various students, and the Tea Ceremony ... Giving this presentation allowed me to review what I had learned about the Japanese and their language.

23 | Unschooling the Arts

At Halloween I wanted to dress up as Max from Maurice Sendak's *Where the Wild Things Are*. I got sidetracked and sat down marveling at *The Art of Maurice Sendak*. On page 22, I ran into the commentary on My Subject:

> 'I hate, loathe, and despise schools,' [says Sendak] ... To this day, he tends to look on all formal education as the sworn enemy of the imagination and its free, creative play ... 'School is bad for you if you have any talent. You should be cultivating that talent in your own particular way.'[17]

This chapter can't teach you to draw gnarly monsters or sing like the wind. Instead, it aims to help you decide how to start cultivating that talent of yours in your own particular way. It can't give in-depth help with everything; it can't even *mention* everything. The arts are endless, especially because artists are always making up new kinds of art.

GENERAL ADVICE

- Find out what your city offers. Call your city council or chamber of commerce and ask them to mail you information on local arts. If you have a center for the performing arts, put your name on their mailing list.
- Don't divorce art from the rest of your life. Remember that decorating your bedroom, planting a garden,

playing your harmonica at sunset, making cards for your friends, painting a mural on the garage, singing a lullaby to your sister, making up dances in your basement and arranging vegetables on a plate are all worthy of your most impassioned artistic efforts. If art does not serve to make life more meaningful, it is empty.

• If you have talent, dedication and a unique approach, you may want to consider going into business as an artist – a photographer or drummer or whatever.

• Try to find a way to share the equipment and space you need through an artist's co-op or through city art programs. Art or craft supply stores are a good place to start asking questions. If you're just starting out in a field, consider going to a class – especially one that lets you come in to use studio space during non-class hours. Once you know what you're doing, look for an apprenticeship that will help you go further.

STUDIO AND FINE ARTS

Check out any local art museums or art centers. Art supply stores are good places to find out about classes and lessons. They are also good places to wander and get inspired by the colors and textures of paints and pens.

Drawing

Realistic drawing skills are necessary for many forms of art, from architecture to sculpture to fashion design as well as making portraits. If you want a class, find one with a live model, preferably nude. Artists need this training to develop a clear sense of the human form.

Photography

If you're serious, find access to a darkroom. Start your search by visiting photo shops and telling them what you're looking for. If you can't find one, consider setting up your own and renting time to other photographers, or else forming a co-op.

Aside from reading good books and magazines, you'll want to look carefully at the work of other photographers. Every once in a while an outstanding photographer writes a book explaining exactly how he or she made certain photographs. One such book is unschooler Ansel Adams's *Examples: The Making of Forty Photographs*.

Film-making and video production

Experiment on your own, analyze other people's films and videos, and hook up with a cable access station. In *GWS* no. 25, Eileen Trombly writes about her unschooled daughter:

> Lori had taken a video course at Connecticut College at the age of 11. Her intense interest in this area caused her to volunteer her services in the filming of several political campaigns in New London, and also for the annual March of Dimes Telerama. She has continued this volunteer work for the last seven years and is now number-one camera person and assistant director for the Telerama. The director from New York phones to be assured of her participation each year. As a result, Lori received a job offer at the Eugene O'Neill Theatre here in Waterford, via the theater director in New York ...

A year and a half later, Lori is in college and Eileen writes again (*GWS* no. 33):

> Lori has already been offered a position at O'Neill for next summer and was given her *own studio* this summer. Even though we're 15 minutes from the theater she sleeps nights at

the mansion provided for the convenience of the NY critics, etc. She often works late hours and is completely immersed in what she does.

Aside from the visual art forms I've mentioned, there are many other applications of artistic skills I don't have room or expertise to discuss. For instance, you can design clothes, do graphic art, make clay pots, design wallpaper or fabric, design small buildings and learn about large-scale architecture, create animated films, sculpt marble angels, or decorate hotels. Os Shepler writes:

> I'm 16 years old and I've been unschooling in Venezuela for six years. Right now I am working towards becoming a full-time comic artist. My journey began when my mother brought home *The Teenage Liberation Handbook*. This book lead me to Barbara Sher's *Wishcraft*, which helped me to name my goal – to create my own comic book – and to break it down into steps and get the support I needed.
>
> I started my search for resources. At first I took general art classes at a small local art studio (in Venezuela extra-curricular activities like art, music, drama and sports are not offered at schools but through private clubs). I was really dissatisfied with the results of my artwork and the amount of discipline I lacked. So, I began writing letters searching for other resources and therefore discovered a series of videos produced by Stan Lee. These videos gave me access to such comic artists as Jim Lee, Todd McFarlane, Rob Liefeld and Will Eisner. I studied these videos inside out and purchased any materials they suggested. I also spent a lot of time studying other comic artists' work. Through this study, I became a comic collector and eventually I started my own business importing comics for other Venezuelan collectors. (Legally, my visa does not permit me to have a paying job, but I may be self-employed.)
>
> Still, my artwork at the time was very poor and disappointing. I knew I needed a mentor. Some unschoolers are very independent and don't depend on the 'mentor' aspect of learning. However, I have discovered that my personal style of learning is very visual and I don't learn very well through

reading books or lectures. I needed someone to show me the process of creating comic art. I tried everything. I wrote a letter to Jim Lee for an apprenticeship, I contacted graduates from Joe Kubert college, I spread the word that I was looking for a mentor in the comic arts. Finally, by some act of God, a fellow missionary friend of my parents found a comic institution in the heart of the city while riding a bus (very *Wishcraft*ish!). She contacted me right away and I immediately put together a portfolio and showed it to the director of the comic institute. They were somewhat impressed and enrolled me in their Venezuelan equivalent of a BA program. When I started my classes, I discovered that at the age of 15 I was the youngest student and that most of the other students were between 18 and 30 years of age.

All my academic subjects are integrated by my endeavor to create my own comic book. I unschool writing by participating in the on-line X-Men Role Playing Game (Uncanny X-MUSH), I learn Spanish by daily use, I learn math through my import business, I created a cartoon character for my Boy Scout troop for environmental science, I do social studies by resolving cross-cultural conflicts in the multi-cultural classroom of my comic school, etc. And Clonlara Home Based Education takes care of documenting all these credits.

At this time, I am pursuing an internship with Marvel Comics because I desire to be familiar with the entire production process. While the industry is experiencing tough times in the United States, in Venezuela it is in crisis! As a student in the Comic Art Institute in Caracas, Venezuela, I and my fellow learners are preparing for careers in an industry which does not exist in this country. Our director and my mentor, Julio Lopez, has told us that the hope for our future depends on a few of us becoming risk-takers and starting a Venezuelan production company and thus providing employment for our fellow artists. I hope to contribute to such an effort.

PERFORMING ARTS

Good performing arts opportunities in school are the exception, not the rule. However, if your school has one of the exceptions, I know better than to tell you it doesn't matter. If your school does have programs you like, find out whether your state or school district allows homeschoolers to participate in extra-curricular activities; many do.

Alternatively, find a program elsewhere – a youth symphony orchestra, a good dance school, a little theater, community musicals, a church choir. Run away and join the circus. And don't rule out college groups. One of my college's modern dance troupes included two school students. No one made a fuss about their age or the fact that they weren't college students; they were welcome because of their seriousness and talent.

You can study or perform by yourself – break dancing on street corners, giving a violin recital, performing stand-up comedy, playing piano in a restaurant. Or team up with friends – as a chamber orchestra, reggae band, tap dance troupe, theater company or circus.

Music

Learn by practicing, experimenting, taking lessons, playing your viola with your favorite songs on the radio, composing, joining the church choir or a big brass band. Stretch your ears by listening to different kinds of music. Try a classical music radio station on Sunday mornings. Public-funded radio stations often offer a wide variety of programs, from traditional Celtic music to Brazilian rock. Phone them and ask them to send you a program guide. Go to concerts. Explore 'alternative' music stores. If you get serious, learn about music theory and composition, through books or tutors or classes.

Fifteen-year-old Saeward Stone of British Columbia, Canada, writes:

Several years ago I began to experiment with making musical instruments. My primary resources were books and imagination. I also began playing the flute. I then found someone in the community who used to make musical instruments professionally, who was happy to work with me. My first project was a mandolin which I was immediately inspired to play. I then made an acoustic guitar. At the moment I am working on a violin, a mandolin for commissioned sale, a rebec, an octave mandolin, another guitar and numerous repairs for people.

I play flute, whistle, mandolin, fiddle and some guitar. My 13-year-old brother plays guitar, piano, five-string banjo and some fiddle. My 10-year-old brother plays fiddle and my 7-year-old sister plays fiddle also. We play a lot of music at dances, song circles, Celtic festivals and at home, calling ourselves 'Stone Circle'. We play folk music – so far, Celtic, Ukrainian and American fiddle tunes.

In the summer we often make $150 an hour busking at the summer market. We are planning to travel to Cape Breton in Canada to participate in music there. My future goals are to build a harpsichord and to travel in Europe to learn more about violin making and music.

Acting

Get involved in local theater, of course, but also think about staging your own play. Libraries have books that explain all the necessary aspects, including directing, set design, lighting, costume design and business concerns. Unschooler Emma Roberts, of Massachusetts, wrote in *GWS* no. 68:

I act a lot in our local community theatre ... This past March I was in *Brighton Beach Memoirs*. I was the only kid under 15 in the cast. Being with all those adults really gave me a professional feeling. The adults were so serious and 50 kids weren't running around making noise. I felt that the play was more realistic than a bunch of kids on stage standing around waiting to say their lines. When I am in a play with other kids I want to hang around and play with the other kids and not really watch the play and pay attention. That is nice too, but I don't feel professional.

Dance

Almost half the unschooled girls who responded to my questionnaire were involved in dance to some degree, and many of them took three or more classes a week. Apart from taking dance lessons, you can audition as a dancer in musicals, start your own troupe, or move to New York to chase the dream of the ballerina. *GWS* no. 30 reprinted part of a newspaper article about Cathy Bergman, former unschooler and president of the National Association of Home Educators:

> Bergman said that as a teenager her goal in life was to be a ballerina. 'I had to practice six hours a day in order to be a ballerina, which I couldn't do if I was at school. In a homeschool I could put all my energies into dance. That doesn't mean I didn't do anything else. When you have so much free time you are inspired to learn and grow. Your interest will lead to another interest. My ballet led to reading about ballet, and that reading gave me history. Reading that history led me to study great figures in art.'

Of course, there is more to dance than ballet, tap, modern and jazz. You can also learn flamenco (fiery controlled passion), international folk dance (lots of intricate footwork), capoeira (Brazilian martial art/dance combination), tai chi (not strictly dance but a graceful Oriental movement focusing on the flow of energy throughout your body), belly dancing (sinuous undulation and intricate hip isolations), classical Indian dance (complex everywhere, especially hands and face), square dancing, ballroom dancing, West African and hula – just to mention a few.

24 | Gym, Mountains, Planet

UNSCHOOLING SPORTS AND FITNESS

What you can do with your body at school is nothing compared to what you can do on an icy hill or a surfboard or a green field or a horse or a bike or a dance floor. If you like playing in sports teams, don't think you can't just because you don't go to school. In many states and countries there are clear allowances for homeschoolers to participate in school sports. In others, there are prohibitions against it. In some, the rules are ambiguous and if you talk to the right people in the right way, you'll be able to play. (I've also heard of homeschoolers in school teams who were considered for sports scholarships.)

But you could also join another team – through a community league, community college, private school or church league. Start your own team of unschoolers and dropouts. Some homeschooling teams join leagues of small private or rural schools. Experiment with coaching yourselves and each other – an excellent experiment in self-directed learning.

Or maybe you're ready to change sports. If you are looking for a new activity, don't think that your only choices are the things you used to do in gym class. Consider walking or biking to work, feisty teenage sports like skateboarding, snowboarding or freestyle biking, yoga, gardening, hiking, climbing, skiing, rollerblading, kayaking, dancing, tai chi, horse riding, martial.arts, trapeze swinging.

MOUNTAINSCHOOLING (AND RIVERSCHOOLING, PRAIRIESCHOOLING, TUNDRASCHOOLING . . .)

Young people growing up now seem far more sophisticated in some ways than my peers and I were as teenagers. For instance, they know and care much more about the world, the environment and people who starve. On the other hand, I see distressing signals that young people are increasingly *softer*, more cautious, overprotected by parents and other adults who don't know them well enough to trust them. I suppose it's also a reflection of our society in general, which at the moment reeks of a squeamish 'better safe than sorry' mentality, with mandatory seatbelt laws, with lawsuits and sanitary codes and endless restrictions. Gumption and bravery are not especially in fashion.

Ignore fashion. Think for yourself. The wilderness does *not* come in a polystyrene package, and you may never make 'sense' of it, but so what? If you proceed with care, you are not going to die or get hurt. Well, you *might*, of course – but it's far more likely you'll die or get hurt in somebody's car. Anyway, neither dying nor getting hurt are anywhere near as unhealthy as avoiding life.

So, do get out and adventure in the wilds, but don't make trouble for yourself by going unprepared. If you don't already have outdoor skills, learn them in the company of people who know what they're doing. Take a first aid course. Choose equipment and clothing carefully so you don't get hypothermia in wet cotton jeans. Don't confuse stupidity with bravery.

Companions and guides

You don't have to take a course to learn outdoor skills any more than you have to go to school to learn history. You can simply tag along with experienced outdoorspeople. If you don't know any, find them by putting up a note on the bulletin boards of outdoor equipment stores or by contacting mountaineering clubs. For trips further afield, hook up via the Internet.

The academic wilderness

You can combine your love of the outdoors with 'academic' study, so that you could spend a whole year on a long-distance trek with Spot and give the school board nothing to complain about. Here are some ideas, but don't go overboard. (I have this horrible vision of wandering through the mountains and stumbling on some teenager who read my book. All around him are strange and magnificent trees. The sun going down splashes eternity everywhere. He sits hunched under a tree, reading a botany textbook, memorizing terms. Then he gets out his *Appreciating Art* book and dutifully studies the paintings of Monet and Van Gogh. Please don't be him.)

Remember that a lot of the beauty of spending time outside is the beauty of simplicity – stripping your life of miscellaneous distractions and conveniences so your soul lies naked, ready to be *touched*. If you are a receptive enough adventurer, you will learn far more from quiet observation than from any contrived academic study. Please keep these things in mind as you read through the following ideas. If you try to incorporate one or two of them into a trip, you may enhance your adventure. If you try to do it all, you might as well just stay home and nail a poster of a wildflower meadow on your door.

- Conduct field research; be a zoologist, ornithologist, botanist or geologist. Collect, observe, experiment. Ask questions: what does the blackbird do if you come closer than 15 feet to its nest? Closer than 10 feet? (But don't

harass.) Record your findings in a notebook.
* Read background information on the area you're in. Ask a ranger station or information center for ideas, or check the bookshelves in a local mountaineering store.
* Paint, sketch or photograph what you see.
* Write it down, following the examples of nature writers like Barry Lopez, Annie Dillard, Ed Abbey and Peter Matthiessen – or romantic poets like Wordsworth, Coleridge and Keats.
* Conduct a bit of sociology during your trips. When you meet someone on the trail, introduce yourself and get their permission to ask questions. Carry out a survey on whatever interests you. Why are they there? Do outdoor experiences make them nicer to their kids? When they are in an empty valley is their belief in a God strengthened or diminished? How, if at all, is their attitude towards the great outdoors different from their attitude toward their own backyard? Write up your results and look for a place to have them published.

Finally, don't shut yourself off from other ways of learning – quiet meditation, fasting, prayer ... *stillness*.

WORLDSCHOOLING

One of the more outrageous unschooling stories is that of Robin Lee Graham, who left school in 1965 at the age of 16 and sailed around the world alone. It took five years and the whole world paid attention. His book *Dove* tells of all kinds of things – battling loneliness and storms, losing a mast, falling in love in the Fiji Islands, feasting on shellfish in the Yasawa Islands and on roast pig and papaya with Savo Islanders, traveling with dolphins and cats, motorcycling through South Africa. When Robin completed his voyage, Stanford University invited him to enroll. He tried it, but left after a term to start a life of self-sufficiency in Montana.

I know people are not used to the idea of teenagers roaming on their own, despite the examples of occasional Robin Grahams. If you totally panic at the thought of exploring strange territory without your mother, independent travel is probably not for you. But if some excitement surges with the panic, maybe you should start fantasizing with maps. No significant legal barriers prevent teenage travel, and if you think you're ready, you are. Yes, tragedy could strike, but no more likely to you than to an adult, and far less likely than if you walked through the halls of most inner city schools.

Why travel?

It's cheaper than private school and far more educational. If you stay in your home country, it can be no more expensive than school plus the food and electricity you consume at home. In *The Next Whole Earth Catalog*, Kevin Kelly wrote, 'The drifters of Europe in the '60s invented a contemporary form of education: extended world travel. At about $3,000 per year, all adventures included, it is still the cheapest college there is.'

I will spare you a big gushy sermon about the joys of travel, since you can make one up for yourself while gazing at any poster of a market in Marrakesh. I *will* say that international traveling is an especially timely thing to do as we shift into a more global economy and awareness.

Travel companions and other informal arrangements

- Join up with other unschoolers through notices in homeschooling publications. In *GWS* no. 35, yacht

owners wrote in seeking a crew member on a cruise through the Caribbean islands, Panama, Seattle and Hawaii.
- Find traveling companions on the Internet.
- Arrange to visit pen pals.
- You can always start traveling on your own, staying in hostels, and then link up with other travelers. If you're female, think carefully about the hazards of being female and alone. However, in many Third World countries while you are likely to be verbally harassed you are unlikely to be physically harmed.

Mixing travel and academic study

Get it through your head that traveling is certainly enough education all by itself. You don't need to cram in scholastic stuff in order to make it meaningful. But a few deliberately added cerebral endeavors *could* intensify your pleasure. Some ideas:

- Go to museums, wherever you are. Art galleries, cultural museums, science museums, history museums. Take your time and remember to forget school-field-trip mode.
- Read about the history, natural history, culture, politics, art or anthropology of the country or state you're visiting.
- Keep a record of your trip in a journal. Consider sharing the journal or adapting it for letters or essays. While unschooler Britt Barker traveled, she described her adventures for her weekly newspaper column back home in Ohio. These columns eventually became a booklet.
- Keep a naturalist's journal of the plants, animals, weather and geology of the areas you visit.

- Take photographs. Capture scenes that most people wouldn't think of recording. Or sketch people, buildings, etc. *Always ask for permission before photographing or sketching people.* Timbuktu is not a zoo.
- Take a tape recorder and conduct oral history interviews. Or use your tape recorder to record the sounds of your trip – a train ride shared with goats and farmers, an evening in the town square with music playing.
- If in a foreign country, speak the language of course. Avoid English and speakers thereof.

Unschoolers at large

In *GWS* no. 52 Dick Gallien writes:

> Just got a call from Linda Salwen of New York … Her homeschooled 14-year-old son found the money, which included $500 from the local paper, to fly with his bike to California where he has started biking *alone* back to New York to raise money for either peace or world hunger … Next year he is planning on biking in Russia.

Unschooler Anita Giesy, of Virginia, spent the equivalent of her last year at school working in a grocery store to make money for the next stage of her education, a year-long trip driving around the country. She wrote a letter to *GWS* about her plans, received around 40 invitations from families to visit, and proceeded to have a wonderful trip, staying five or six days with each family. To other young travelers, she advises that the most important thing is to be adaptable, to consider it all an opportunity to learn. 'As long as you don't have any particular expectations,' she says, 'everything that happens is a bonus.' Anita gave me an article she'd written for a homeschooling newsletter. Part of it says:

> So I planned it all out and on 8 September 1990 I set off on my great journey. From Virginia, I went criss-crossing the south out

to California, staying with homeschooling families all the way. I've been as far south as Florida and New Orleans. Before I'm done, I'll go as far north as Vancouver in Canada. The families have been wonderful and I've been able to live, work and play with them. The first family I stayed with, the father was a potter. The day after I arrived was clay-mixing day and I helped mix one ton of clay. I stayed with a midwife and got to attend a birth. I stayed with a college art teacher and was a model for his art class. Every family is a new opportunity to learn and make new friends. And I guess you could say, I've gone from a homeschooler to a worldschooler.

25 | College without School[1]

YES, UNSCHOOLERS CAN GO TO COLLEGE

Among the hundreds of colleges and universities in the US that have admitted homeschoolers are Amherst, Antioch, Boston University, Brigham Young University, Caltech, Carleton, Carnegie-Mellon University, the College of William and Mary, Colorado College, Duquesne University, Evergreen, Harvey Mudd, MIT, Michigan Technological University, Northwestern University, Oberlin, Princeton, Rice University, St John's, Sarah Lawrence, Swarthmore, Texas A and M, Wellesley, West Point, the US Naval Academy, the US Air Force Academy, the University of Pennsylvania, Williams and Yale. In the UK, colleges in Oxford and Cambridge, and York University have admitted homeschoolers. In Japan, at least two universities have admitted homeschoolers. Homeschoolers have gone onto various four-year colleges, two-year colleges, and art and trade schools in other countries, including Canada, Mexico, Scotland, Ireland, Australia, and New Zealand. And as the homeschooling movement in other countries gains momentum, good news begins to trickle in from around the globe.[18]

1 Note to readers ouside the US: In this book, the term 'college' is meant in the American sense: like a university, it is an institution for higher education usually attended by people approximately 18 to 22 years of age. (Colleges are generally smaller and sometimes more specialized than universities.)

Indeed, the question is no longer 'Can unschoolers get into college?' but rather 'How can unschoolers best and most clearly present themselves to college admissions departments?' The cutting-edge pioneers in college admissions are no longer unschoolers, but rather unschooling test resisters – that is, people who refuse to take standardized entry tests.

Back in 1990, when fewer homeschoolers had grown up and applied to college, I put the following question to the admissions directors of America's most selective, respected universities and liberal art colleges:

... If an applicant to [Barnard, etc.] had completed little or no formal schooling, would you still consider her? I am not talking here about the stereotypical teenage dropout, but rather a creative, enterprising individual who has done one or several interesting things with her time, such as started a business, played in a jazz band, traveled, written comic books, volunteered in Greenpeace, or raised boa constrictors. I also mean someone who has taken care to meet your admissions requirements through other means than attending school – studied English, mathematics, foreign languages, science and social science on her own or with a tutor, and taken achievement tests as well as college entry tests demonstrating that she performs just as well as your successful applicants ...

Of the 27 admissions directors and officers who responded, none said no, although three were skeptical. Most said that they would be completely open to such applicants, but didn't want their openness to be misinterpreted as welcoming people who had merely 'done their own thing' for several years and not bothered to learn mathematics or strong writing skills. Some were already accustomed to the idea and warmly positive. But all agreed, with varying levels of enthusiasm, that they'd willingly consider such an applicant.

So, take encouragement from the optimistic admissions officers and learn from the pessimists. If you want to go to a selective college, know what it takes. It may be safe to say that being unschooled makes your application stand out, but it will *not* make up for what they consider a weak academic background.

Also, be ready to educate confused or hesitant admissions people. Tell them explicitly what you have been up to, and take the initiative to correct misconceptions politely. Remember that the homeschooling movement is still young, so college people haven't yet had the chance to see much of what it's about.

Most admissions people were quite positive. For instance, Mark F Silver, Associate Director of Undergraduate Admissions at Washington University, writes

> My first response to reading your letter was: 'Where is this student? Does he or she exist? How can we get him or her to apply to Washington University?' I am being somewhat facetious; however, the short answer to your question is that we would most definitely be interested in hearing from a student such as you describe in your letter. We have never stood on standard, traditional preparation as the sole criterion for admission. As a matter of fact, a number of [such] students, many from homeschooled situations, have been evaluated and admitted ...
>
> There are many factors that indicate success in college for prospective students, and academic achievement in a traditional setting is but one. Leadership skills, ability to cope with new and different situations, the ability to synthesize information in creative ways, and a person's intense interest in a specific field all add to the likelihood of their success at college. I often encourage students with whom I speak during my recruiting activities to consider taking a year off between school and college to enhance just those skills.

Will unschooling affect your ability to get into college? Probably not. If you were on the path to Oxford when you were in school, you can stay on it out of school. If you were planning to go to a technical or community college, those doors remain open also. What may change: you will probably become a more interesting, skilled and knowledgeable person, one whom selective colleges will find more enticing. Or your values may change and you may decide to work toward something besides college.

COLLEGE NOW

An interesting side issue of the unschooling/college question is the possibility of beginning college at an early age. Many unschoolers find that while school is indeed a waste of time, college skips the busywork and has time to get to the point and beyond it. In fact, this was a recurring pattern among the teenagers who described their lives to me. They frequently led very unstructured, unpressured lives without school, which gave them freedom in which to develop one or more intense interests. Thus, by the time they were 14, 15, 16 or 17, many wanted to participate in a challenging, meaningful, academic (but not school) environment.

Many unschoolers begin their college careers by taking one or two courses through universities or community colleges, while otherwise continuing their unstructured, teenage lives. Leonie Edwards, who began working as a dental assistant at age 14, also began earning college credits through correspondence courses which will apply toward her pre-dental coursework.

HOW YOUR MATURE, UNSCHOOLED PERSPECTIVE WILL INFLUENCE YOUR COLLEGE EXPERIENCE

First of all, it will help you get into college. Maturity always does. But it will also help immeasurably once you're there.

By leaving school ahead of the crowd, especially if you take yourself out into the world, you give yourself a most valuable clear head, a feeling for truth and reality that just doesn't happen until you're away from the world of intellectual guidance for a while. With that perspective, all your decisions will be wiser – including the major decisions whether to attend college, where to attend college and what to study.

BUT DO YOU REALLY WANT TO GO TO COLLEGE?

I wish someone had asked me this question, in a serious tone of voice. At our house it was assumed that one goes to college, and Not Just Any College but a Reputable and Highly Esteemed one. Had I noticed that I didn't have to go, maybe I wouldn't have. Maybe I would have, but with clearer expectations.

Why do you want to attend college? Will college give you what you want? Are there other ways to get what you want? There are certainly excellent things about college, and most uglinesses of school have no twins in college. Nevertheless, if you go to college without ever thinking about the possibility of not going to college, it takes on many of the same negative qualities as 'compulsory' school. *Don't enroll just because it's expected of you.*

Here are a couple of other perspectives to encourage you to think about whether you want a degree. Thirteen-year-old Anne Brosnan wrote to me:

> I really don't know if I'm going to college or not. I might win a scholarship somewhere. I might be busy. I might be canoeing in Canada or selling hammocks in Hawaii. It all depends. My plans for the future are to maybe be a pianist (therefore I might go to a music college) or a writer/poet (therefore I don't really need to go to college). I could do a lot of things. I also want to have a farm. That's easily accomplished without a college

education, especially if you can teach yourself agriculture just like you did school subjects.

Anne Herbert writes in 'The Rising Sun Neighborhood Newsletter' in *The Next Whole Earth Catalog*:

> I've noticed that when I meet people my own age who seem to have had a truly incredible number of adventures, they turn out to have not gone to college, so instead of doing one thing for four years they started doing two or three things a year as soon as they left school.

Realize that while a college degree definitely makes many *jobs* easier to get, unschooling all the way through your life probably makes it easier for you to make a living out of the things you love. Almost anything can become an independent business, whether in environmental consultation or in teaching and performing with steel drums. If you open up your head you can open up your life. Rather than go to college and graduate school to become a marine biologist, for instance, you could go straight to the coast of British Columbia at the age of 18, begin conducting your own research on salmon spawning (investing far less money than you would in college) and, by the time you were 22 or 23, you'd probably look far more appealing than laboratory rat-people to the powers who hire marine biologists. Of course, by that time you might have come up with ways of making your research pay you without having an employer. You might even be hiring your own laboratory rat-people.

Instead of college, you could just get on with life – or you could design your own course of study, unschooling your way through college. Kendall Hailey did just that and wrote a book called *The Day I Became An Autodidact*. If you want to unschool on a high academic level, I strongly recommend using *The Independent Scholar's Handbook* by Ronald Gross, a thorough guide to conducting intellectual projects without being a student, professor or research assistant.

Finally, just as there are lists of people who accomplish all manner of wonders without going to school, there are even longer lists of people who succeed spectacularly without college. As you'd expect, many of them are artists and writers, but they also include scientists such as Jane Goodall, who had no university degree, nor any formal training in ethology, when she began her work with chimpanzees in Tanzania. (After she'd been at it for five years, however, she wrote a thesis and Cambridge awarded her a doctorate.) Steve Jobs and Stephen Wozniak, founders of Apple Computers, dropped out of college. Physicist/architect/generalist extraordinaire Buckminster Fuller was expelled from Harvard. A few other people on the uncolleged list include Ernest Hemingway, Paul Gauguin, Amelia Earhart, Eleanor Roosevelt, Harry S Truman, Lewis Mumford, Ralph Lauren, Robert Frost, Walt Disney, Charles Schultz and Roger Tory Peterson.[19]

GETTING INTO UNITED STATES STATE UNIVERSITIES AND COMMUNITY COLLEGES[2]

Admission to most US community colleges and many state universities is a fairly cut and dried process. You will probably have to take the GED and pass it. Each state has a minimum age requirement for the GED, often 18.

2 Note to non-US readers: The information in this section and the next section ('Getting into selective colleges and universities') is written from a US perspective. However, many of the same principles will apply to homeschoolers in other countries. You should also speak with local homeschoolers, who may know more about the situation where you live. If you are confused or anxious about this issue, one of the best strategies is to enroll with Clonlara, the respected international long-distance 'school' for unschoolers. Clonlara's diplomas and credentials are accepted and legal in many countries – see the resource list at the end of this book.

Homeschoolers are working to abolish this minimum age requirement, but in the meantime you can often get special permission from a school board to take it sooner. Ask local homeschoolers whether they know of anyone who has been able to take it at an early age. For information on registering for the test, contact a library, high school or community college. GWS no. 27 offers this story:

> Last February, our daughter (16) became impatient at having to wait till she was 18 to take her GED test and start her course at the Technical Institute (she has decided she wants to be an astronaut!). So she talked me into appealing to the school superintendent for permission to take the GED before reaching the required age ... As soon as he understood our request he said he would be happy to oblige, and that was that.

You may not even need to take the GED. Most major universities do have some kind of clause in their admissions requirements that leaves room for admitting students with 'special circumstances'. Of course, if an epidemic of unschooling breaks out (go team!), your circumstances will no longer be special. But having to take the GED is painless compared to having to take six years' worth of school, including a few too many unimaginative exams. If there's a specific university you hope to attend, write to their admissions department and ask whether they have any specific guidelines for homeschoolers.

GETTING INTO UNITED STATES SELECTIVE COLLEGES AND UNIVERSITIES

These institutions want their incoming students to have a broad, thorough education. Normally, they measure this education mainly by looking at high school transcripts. Their verdict also depends heavily on recommendations from teachers or other adults, on an application essay, on the strength of one's 'extra-curricular' interests and achievements, on standardized test scores, and sometimes on an interview.

Do your best to see the admissions process through the eyes of admissions officers. When an admissions officer looks at your unschoolish application, her job will instantly grow both more interesting and more confusing. Without the standard transcript of courses and grades, she will need assurance of some other variety that you are a strong candidate. The more clearly you show what you know, what you can do and how you've spent your time, the sweeter her job will be. As Paul Thiboutot, Dean of Admissions at Carleton, points out, he prefers students with traditional backgrounds because this background 'gives us the easiest means for evaluating readiness to pursue college study'. Admissions people have incredible paperwork, and if tons of you descend on them all at once, it will be difficult for them to be happy about it. Don't be their logistical nightmare.

Nevertheless, colleges are increasingly prepared to deal with nonstandard applications. The admissions director at Washington University says:

> Our only concern in evaluating such individuals has been: are they prepared to meet the academic demands of Washington University? ... We would rely on standardized testing, AP or Achievement tests to evaluate their academic preparation. On those rare occasions that students approaching your description have applied to us, we have often requested a formal interview on campus.

Of course, despite the headaches you will cause, you can also delight admissions people. Set yourself apart from the masses who are only applying to college because it's the next step in a routine they've never thought about. Make the people who read your application feel honored that you *want* to be at their institution – even though you know from experience that you could choose to learn independently instead.

And make their fears go away. Unless they have had some positive experience in the unschooling department, admissions people may be full of all the worst stereotypes about homeschoolers. They may suspect you of not having any social skills, or of never having heard of Darwin, or of not being able to do much algebra.

More reasonably, they may be concerned that you will have a difficult time adjusting to a structured learning environment which other people direct. Delsie Z Phillips, Director of Admissions at Haverford, speaks for many when she says:

> The academic program at Haverford is structured, and the faculty give grades. There are not other options. It would be important to us to know that the student understands this and is truly seeking the kind of educational framework we provide.

If you don't want to be in college, you *will* have a difficult time. Don't be mistaken as to why these colleges exist. Don't feel that they owe you places in their classrooms and laboratories. Don't think they should accept you because you're an interesting person and then let you do whatever you feel like doing. By enrolling, you are agreeing to play their game. Their game is a good one. But there are other good games.

Most colleges base admissions on transcripts, an application essay, test scores, references, extracurricular activities and sometimes an interview. Unschoolers differ from schoolers mainly on their references and transcripts.

References

You will need at least two letters from adults who know you and believe in you. If you were at school, these people would probably be teachers. If you're not, they won't be. Instead, employers or mentors do nicely. Sarah Pitts, of Georgia, went on to Boston College. In *GWS* no. 96, she says:

> It's a good idea to plan ahead and get letters from anyone outside the family with whom you have extended contact, even when you're young. If you get involved with an activity when you're 14 and do it for a year, it may be hard to find that person years later when you're applying to college. When I was about 15 I worked as a counselor with my county 4-H group (a US youth organization). At the end of the summer the counselor wrote me a letter thanking me, and we copied that and sent it to the colleges. It would have been hard to track her down later if I hadn't got the letter at the time.

In lieu of the high school transcript

Most colleges will want you to provide a clear, concise outline of your academic work for the past four years or so; many families create 'transcripts' as if they actually ran a little school at home. In some cases, that won't be enough.

After hearing from both admissions officers and unschooled teenagers, I strongly advise: before you apply to a selective college, take at least one course through a local university or community college. This way, you both prove that you can handle college-level, structured coursework *and* find out cheaply whether you *like* doing it. Bowdoin Director of Admissions, William R Mason, commented:

> We have two students entering this year … who were completely homeschooled. Each of them did take local college courses and the support from teachers was exceptional enough to convince us that both these students possess superior academic ability.

If your application is scanty, a selective college may even

ask you to start by enrolling elsewhere full time. For instance, Delsie Z Phillips of Haverford says, 'In some cases we have asked students who lack formal education and testing to enroll in an open admission college to prove their ability to excel in a structured situation. When they have presented appropriate grades, we admit them.'

PART 4 | Touching the World – Finding Good Work

26 | Beyond Fast Food

I want to be thoroughly used up when I die, for the harder I
work the more I live. I rejoice in life for its own sake.

George Bernard Shaw

Equipping yourself academically certainly won't take all
your time, and this world needs your contribution. We are
starved for people who work with not just their hands and
their minds, but also with their hearts. Most teenagers crave
the chance to do real work – something that makes a
difference in the world – instead of sitting and taking notes
all day. Some work brings money, some doesn't. I'm going
to talk about the kind that doesn't as much as the kind that
does. You should try to think of work as something that
matters – not just a way to sell your time, body and soul in
return for cash. John Holt came up with a healthy definition
in *Teach Your Own*: 'By "work" I ... mean ... what people
used to call a "vocation" or "calling" – something which
seemed so worth doing for its own sake that they would
gladly choose to do it even if they didn't need money and
the work didn't pay.'

NOW VERSUS LATER

When I was a teenager I hated the nonsense question adults
asked: 'And what do you want to do with your life?' Like
the other standard 'Do you like school?' it made no sense to

me. It referred to some abstract future instead of my present. I always had answers, but my heart wasn't in them. At the time, all I really knew was that I had to go to school, supposedly so that I could later apply my school knowledge to whatever I did. Unfortunately, it didn't occur to me that I could also have begun doing the things that I dreamed about doing 'some day'.

In your unschooled life, the question of good work is a question about your here and now, not just a speculation about your future. In ten years, you may change your mind completely about everything, including what work you want. If that happens, you can get the skills and knowledge you need then. Your task now is to use your time beautifully *now*. Your life isn't something that's going to start happening when you're 21. It's happening today. In fact, one of the great things about unschooling is that it makes healthy future work much more likely. It allows your present to blend with your future, with no forced split.

HOW TO BE READY FOR MONDAY

Do work you love. You *can* do work you love. Enjoy your distinct advantage over adults. Unless your parents are the vindictive kind who say 'go to school or get a job and pay your way', you aren't yet pressured to be financially independent. (If your parents do hint in that direction, remind them that the whole idea of education, in school or elsewhere, depends on children not being forced to earn money. You need time to explore, which is why you left school in the first place.) In other words, part of your education can be doing terrific work even if it doesn't pay for your meals. Adults who have to buy the tofu don't have that luxury.

Of course, you might start a silkscreening business at 15 which succeeds spectacularly. Or you might begin volunteer work which leads directly to happy employment a year from now. But you can also do work that might *never* bring dollar bills – spending Tuesday mornings at a battered women's shelter, organizing a talent show, planting trees or a garden, teaching your mother how to use a computer.

START SHORT

When you approach businesses or adults – looking for apprenticeships, internships, volunteer opportunities or jobs – sometimes you're more likely to coax a 'yes' out of them if you suggest a trial period. As Emily Bergson-Shilcock says in *GWS* no. 95:

> Almost everything we do, we say, 'Let's try it for three weeks first.' It's easier for people to say yes that way. If you walk into a store and say, 'I'd like to volunteer here', and they've never had volunteers before, it's more likely that they'll say no. Just because they haven't had volunteers, that doesn't mean they can't, but it's easier for them to say yes to something short term. Then if it works out, you can keep going ... In a lot of ways it's easier to go into a smaller business, and easier if you already know and like the people.

TRY A CLASS OR PROGRAM

If suggesting a trial period doesn't work, sometimes it helps to enroll in a class or other program at the business or organization where you'd like to volunteer, work, apprentice, or intern. That's just another way to get your foot in the door, and to get to know the staff and let them get to know you.

DOING IT

The possibilities, of course, are exhilaratingly endless, but to help you begin thinking I've grouped many of them into categories: apprenticeships, internships, volunteering, jobs and businesses. Remember, you don't have to model your working pattern on typical adult working patterns. You can combine several jobs or activities. You needn't do one thing for 40 hours a week. Here are a couple of stories that show the variety that's possible in one life. Lavonne Bennett writes in *GWS* no. 18 about her son, a 'mechanical and electronics genius' described as a 'stupid dummy' by a schoolteacher:

> We took him out of high school in the middle of his junior year … He's 17 now and has managed two stores for an electronics-product firm, renovated a $150 wreck and made it into a classic sports car, has bought equipment for his recording studio, has been a mentor for an 8-year-old boy, helping him to organize model-train layouts, and has given guitar lessons.

Ann Martin from England tells about her son Nicholas, 14, in *GWS* no. 21:

> He spends one afternoon [each week] in a shoe workshop where he helps out in exchange for tuition and will bring home his own hand-made shoes next week! He has been on a residential sports course, goes on trips with a local theatre company, and he helps in a shop owned by a friend of mine, who is teaching him the basic skills of running a business.

27 | Apprenticeships and Internships

A great many of the people who are doing serious work in the world (as opposed to just making money) are very overworked, and short of help. If a person, young or not so young, came to them and said, 'I believe in the work you are doing and want to help you do it in any and every way I can, will do any kind of work you ask me to do or that I can find to do, for very little pay or even none at all,' I suspect that many or most of them would say, 'Sure, come right ahead.' Working with them, the newcomer would gradually learn more and more about what they were doing, would find or be given more interesting and important things to do, might before long become so valuable that they would find a way to pay her/him. In any case, s/he would learn far more from working with them and being around them than s/he could have learned in any school or college.

John Holt, *Growing Without Schooling* no. 6

Apprenticeships and internships can take place in any field, from chemistry research to interior decorating. They build on the concept of mutual benefit. The apprentice or intern gives labor in exchange for the chance to learn about a certain kind of work. The labor itself may seem repetitive or boring to someone experienced in the field, but should be interesting and educational for a newcomer. By the same token, the 'master' or supervisor should not have to take a lot of time to stop and explain how to do things, because the apprentice will learn mainly by watching and doing. Sometimes the apprentice or intern is also paid in money, sometimes not. Sometimes the apprentice or intern pays a little bit. Most often, no money is exchanged. What's the difference between internships and apprenticeships? Internships often involve office or administrative work, while apprenticeships usually focus on learning specific skills in a craft or trade. But many people use the terms interchangeably.

For nationwide and planetwide opportunities, check your library for a reference book like *Internships: on-the-job training opportunities for college students and adults*. You'll find thousands of listings in communications, arts, human services, public affairs, science, industry and other areas. Some positions offer stipends. Many provide room and board, free classes, college credit and help with finding employment after you finish the internship. The majority say that their established internship positions are open only to college students. However, many are open to school-age people. Furthermore, almost all organizations are open to 'independent' inquiries. In other words, they will consider ignoring normal requirements, possibly creating special positions for people who wouldn't fit into their usual internships. And anyway, persevering unschoolers often find that age requirements are not written in stone.

Remember that less famous organizations will be easier to break into. A small town newspaper, for instance, won't have as many applicants as *The Washington Post* or *The Times*.

Your library may also have more specialized apprenticeship or internship guides, like Ronald W Fry's *Internships: Newspaper, Magazine, and Book Publishing*.

HOW YOU CAN ARRANGE AND DESIGN YOUR OWN APPRENTICESHIP OR INTERNSHIP

You may need perseverance, but all you really have to do is decide what kind of a position you want, and then talk to everyone in your area who works in that field until you find someone you like who will take you on.

You'll have it easiest if you already have adult friends you might like to apprentice yourself to, or if your parents know someone who might work out. But of course you can approach strangers too. After all, apprenticeships and internships help everyone involved. You learn by watching people who know what they're doing and by actually doing many of the same things they do. They get free or inexpensive help, as well as the joy and pride that comes from sharing what they love with an excited newcomer. Chances are, if you phone all the dog trainers in the telephone directory, at least one will let you try a one-day experiment, and that may lead into a week-long job, and then a three-month apprenticeship. Don't give up after one 'no-thank you'.

If you do arrange an apprenticeship or internship on your own, be sure to talk about your ideas and goals thoroughly enough that both parties have similar expectations. Write them down. If you envision three hours on weekday mornings of laying out newspaper copy, but Mr Mendoza sees you sweeping floors and running errands, it won't work. Discover that *before* you commit yourself.

FOR EXAMPLE

Anna-Lisa Cox of Michigan wrote about the process of developing an interest in historical costume and finding a related internship. First, in *GWS* no. 68 she says:

> I am 17, and until I became a part-time student at the local college a couple of years ago, I had been schooled at home all my life.
>
> My main passion in life right now is, and has been for the last three years, social anthropology and history. Antique

clothing has been the context which brought these subjects alive for me. I became interested in antique clothing when I was living in England for a year with my family. I stumbled upon the Victoria and Albert Museum in London, which has one of the best costume collections in Europe. I was instantly fascinated by it, and I determined to find out more about the subject.

Now, three years later, I have a large costume collection of my own (acquired through hours of rummaging through charity shops, garage sales, and local estate sales), which I use in historical fashion presentations for local clubs, churches, and businesses. I am also the costume collection consultant for the local historical society. I find what I do very exciting. It's wonderful to be able to help friends date their grandmother's dress, or to teach them how to clean and preserve it ...

A year later, she writes in *GWS* no. 74,

My true love is museum work, tied to an intense interest in antique clothing. Luckily, my parents have been an incredible help and encouragement, patiently supporting me in my exploration and decision-making ...

With the help of friends I was able to find [a museum internship], which I will be going to in April. Some friends arranged for me to get together with the curators of a costume museum near them. I was a little hesitant about even trying, as I had been disappointed so many times, but I decided to go ahead, and I'm so glad I did. The curators are three young women, all as excited and interested in costume as I am. When I first met them we talked for two hours straight. Around the end of our conversation, the head museum curator asked what museum I was in charge of! I decided to tell her the truth, that I had no museum experience, but she said she was very impressed with my expertise and would still love to have me come and work with them.

It all sounds so easy as I write about it, but getting to this point has taken enormous amounts of time and energy. In fact, last summer, when I was in England with my family, I went through an intensive search for an internship. I wrote and called museums. I even had a friend who used to be a costume curator helping me, writing letters of recommendation to old colleagues. But even so, not one internship came out of it. So I guess all I can recommend is to keep trying. There's an internship out there just waiting for you, if you have patience.

At 15, Tad Heuer of Massachusetts spent a summer working as a legislative intern. Like most legislative interns, Tad did his share of grunge work – typing names and addresses into databases, sorting the mail, etc. But many aspects of the work were interesting. In *GWS* no. 98, he writes:

When people had questions about bills, I would get a copy of the bill and additional information from the committee where it had been sent for review. This information went to Rep. Gardner, who gave me her position and an outline of a possible reply. I then wrote a letter to the constituent. When people requested information about laws, I would call the department that was most likely to have jurisdiction.

The Senate Legislative Education Office sponsored intern seminars almost every day. These were one of the best parts of my internship. They were given by representatives, senators, lobbyists, press secretaries, etc. They spoke on a variety of issues and always gave us a chance to ask questions. One speaker discussed Hydro-Quebecois II's plans to flood Cree Indian land to create a massive power grid for the Northeastern US. Another told us about the first bill he introduced. It called for all deer killed by cars to be frozen and distributed to homeless shelters for stew meat! (It passed overwhelmingly.) The seminars were also a good place to meet other interns. Before each seminar, we had to stand up and introduce ourselves. Although all the other interns were college students, they were very friendly and didn't treat me differently because of my age.

Working as an intern was a wonderful introduction to the world of politics. Besides learning about the day-to-day life of legislators, I also improved my communication skills ...

28 | Volunteering

'Volunteer work is a tremendous use of time,' 17-year-old former unschooler Anthony Hermans told me. 'It accomplishes a useful task, allows one to get away from the norm and provides many longlasting friendships. I have volunteered in community service clubs, at the local library, our wildlife sanctuary, and a local history reenactment park. My sister has helped at a local homeless shelter for women and children.'

Two big thrills come with volunteer work: the knowledge that you are helping something you believe in, and a huge realm of possibilities. Volunteering can be *anything*, a free ticket into any world you want to explore. Also, you can set your own schedule, working as much or as little as you wish. Few groups will turn you away because of your age. Volunteer experience looks great on a résumé, and furthermore, volunteer jobs often turn into paid jobs.

In my city, I can think of a wide variety of organizations largely staffed by volunteers: the senior citizens' support system, the soup kitchen, the Humane Society, a non-profit Latin American import shop. Every city has its own counterparts to these, and there are also branches of environmental, social and political action groups – Greenpeace, the Sierra Club, Amnesty International, the Greens, the Republicans, the Democrats.

But you're not restricted to the groups that actively search for volunteers. You can always go to an organization, person or business you like and speak your piece – 'I'd like to get involved with what you're doing. Is there something I can do to help, for free?' or 'I'm a mime; I'd like to teach a free weekly class at the Immigration Center.'

FOR EXAMPLE

A parent writes in *GWS* no. 36:

> Since spring, our 13-year-old daughter has been volunteering at a science museum two days a week. To say that she loves it is an understatement! She's been doing a great deal of work in the museum's 'mount room', cataloging their collections and learning names (in scientific as well as laypeople's terms) of many birds and mammals in the process ... She's becoming quite the birder. Occasionally she gets to go on a field trip with the museum's naturalist. And we all got to go (at special staff rates) on a whale watch sponsored by the museum ...
>
> The naturalist, by the way, has been very impressed by both of our children's obvious love of and knowledge of nature. He said that he'd be more than happy to take them out into the field any time. All the museum staff thinks that it's wonderful that our daughter had the chance to be doing this and have been very supportive, giving her a range of things to do to broaden her experiences there. Occasionally she will take over for the receptionist, and the accountant wants to teach her some of that. She can use the cash register and she helps get out mailings at times. Everyone has found out what a good worker she is and the demand has become high! Her major focus is and will be, at her request, the natural history work.

Twelve-year-old Frank Conley writes in *GWS* no. 30:

> I am presently doing a veterinary medicine course at Louisiana State University. (This course is being given for 'gifted and talented' junior high and high school students – I had no trouble registering as a homeschooler.) I became interested in learning more about it and decided to ask a local veterinarian

if I could help out at his clinic in return for the experience of watching them work.

It has been very worthwhile. The three vets who work there have been very kind and helpful to me. They explain everything they do and not only allow me to watch but actually let me perform certain duties. They say I'm 'indispensable'.

So far some of the most interesting things I've done are: watch an autopsy on a cat, learn to draw blood from animals and prepare slides, take temperatures and fecals, watch surgery performed, and go along on emergency calls.

I go to the clinic nearly every day now, for several hours a day. I plan to take an animal science course next. I recommend this way of learning to everyone. At first I was afraid no one would want my help, since I'm only 12, but the people I talked to were happy to have free help ...

Karen Franklin of Florida wrote in *GWS* no. 72:

Adam, our 12-year-old, spends a lot of time at the Science Museum ... Adam's big interest is marine biology, especially sharks. The director of the museum is an expert on this, has worked with the top people in the field. The main exhibition this summer was about sharks, so Adam, already quite an expert, led many tours and answered many questions.

Seventeen-year-old Sarabeth Matilsky of New Jersey writes,

There's definitely never a dull moment at the George Street Co-op, the store that has been the hub of my family's community since before I can remember. The co-op has been much more than a food store for us – it has been a place to meet people, to socialize, to network, to learn. I started working in the store by myself when I was 9 (to fulfill my family's work requirements), and when I was 13 I got my own membership. Over the years I've worked hundreds of hours in the co-op, doing my own hours, other people's hours, and sometimes just working all day when there were no volunteers and the coordinator was going crazy. I have always felt respected while working in the

store, if not always by strangers shopping ('You're *what?*...
Only *12 years old??*') then certainly by the staff and most of the
other members I've worked with.

As I've gotten older and more experienced, I've been offered
more and more responsibility. On any given day that I come in
to work I may stock shelves, price grocery items, package bulk
food, stock from the overstock areas, package produce, fill
pasta bins, bring food down from the upstairs freezer, scrub the
floor, check in orders, run the register, organize refrigerators,
process special orders, or do any other of the million and one
things that need to be done in order to operate a retail store.
While doing these things I've learned many varied and useful
skills, such as: understanding the math that's involved when
members get their various discounts at the register, dealing
with fussy shoppers, understanding the behind-the-scenes
stuff that happens in a food store, including budget
management from year to year and the nuances of profit
margins, plus countless other things. The co-op has been an
invaluable part of my education – not just because it's taught
me about politics or social studies or math or geography, but
because it's helped me learn *all* that and more. It hasn't been
my school or college education, but rather a part of my *life*
education.

29 | Jobs

I was like many other fullbloods. I didn't want a steady job in an office or factory. I thought myself too good for that, not because I was stuck up but simply because any human being is too good for that kind of no-life, even white people ...

John Fire (Lame Deer), *Lame Deer, Seeker of Visions*

Don't be limited by the stereotypes that tell us what kinds of jobs teenagers can do. You can do more than babysit, flip pancakes and wash cars. Jobs in specialty retail stores, for example, are one of the best ways to get involved in a field that you love. Consider comic-book stores, pet stores, bookstores, jewelry stores, imported clothing stores, antique stores, feed stores, bike shops, cheese stores, bakeries, natural foods stores, piano stores, record stores. The people who work in these places are often very knowledgeable, and you will learn from being around them and the 'stuff' itself. Also, retail stores frequently hire teenagers.

Or consider looking for work through your parents' network of friends or through the homeschool community. *GWS* often runs advertisements or announcements of homeschooling families who want a teenaged live-in nanny.

Know about the child labor statutes in your state or country so you can figure out how to work around them, and when you need to be low key. Generally, in the US you have to be 14 to get a work permit; employers are supposed to keep these permits on file for any employees under 18. You may have to get a permit through the counseling office of your ex-school. Some homeschoolers' employers, however, have only requested written permission from parents. In general in the US, both state and federal laws influence your situation. For more information, contact your state or region labor (employment) department (look in the phone book), or call local representatives and ask them to send you copies of the regulations.

If you are especially young or have difficulty getting a job, consider offering to work for very low wages – but only at first. Once you're good at your job, don't feel embarrassed to ask to be paid more; if you work as well as an adult does, you deserve an adult wage. If you are legal and have a work permit, then in many countries you are entitled to minimum wage, no matter how old you are. If you feel you're being taken advantage of, discuss it with your boss. If that doesn't work, contact your department of labor for information and help.

Another alternative, which need not be demeaning or unfair, is to work for trade (in exchange for something other than money). If you are quite young, this could make the whole situation easier on your employer, who could call you an apprentice or a volunteer and thus avoid trouble with tax people and labor department people.

You-the-unschooler have an edge on the best summer jobs, including jobs at camps, resorts and national parks, because such places prefer people who can work the whole season – often May to September, not just June to August. Check the library for books on summer jobs for teenagers and college students.

FOR EXAMPLE

Erin Roberts, 14, of Maryland, wrote to me about her work with horses. She has worked part time at a riding stable for four years, guiding trail rides and otherwise helping out. She also works at an Arabian farm, Windsor Arabians, as an assistant trainer. 'I especially help break their three- and four-year olds,' she explains, 'but I also help out with halter breaking the young ones as well as miscellaneous tasks around the farm.' She recently bought a three-year-old halter-broken Arabian gelding and trained him to ride. When I heard from her, they had just entered their first show and Erin said, 'We didn't win any ribbons, but we had a great time.'

Scott Maher, 13, of Massachusetts, writes in *GWS* no. 37:

In September I went down to the Wakefield Pet Shop and asked the owner Steve, whom I already knew, if there would be any way I could come down and help. I told him how I was a homeschooler and that I could come down in the mornings. Steve said we could try it out for a while and see what we thought.

I went down on a Monday at 10:30 and first he showed me around and showed me how things are done ... I started off feeding the birds and cleaning their cages. Next I swept the floor and fed the fish. Then I fed and watered the small animals, lizards, rabbits, guinea pigs and cats. Some days I clean filters in the fish tanks and test the pH of the water; other days I clean the cages and clean the glass. I have helped unload shipments and put stock away.

I have been working there almost four months now. I have waited on customers, given them advice, taken inventory and I even take care of the shop if Steve has to leave. Soon I will be learning how to use the cash register.

I think the best part of it is learning about all of the different animals, fish and birds and learning how to take care of them. I have been put in charge of lizards and small animals. It is a lot of fun to help out customers.

A year later, Mary Maher, Scott's mother, sent an update to
GWS no. 43:

> There have been many times when Steve, the owner, has
> called Scott at home and asked him to please come down for
> the day because he very much needed his help. On several
> occasions, Steve has had to leave the store for several hours
> and he has left Scott alone, in charge. When Steve opened a
> second pet shop in a nearby city, he often took Scott with him
> at night to get things unpacked or to set up displays or even
> to have Scott help put up paneling and install ceilings. Once
> in a while, Scott travels with Steve in the evenings to service
> or set up very large fish tanks for restaurants or private
> residences.
>
> Customers don't seem to mind that Scott is so young. They
> will engage him in lengthy conversations on how to take care
> of a particular pet or how to go about properly setting up a fish
> tank. One fellow, an older man, took all Scott's advice on what
> fish were compatible for his new tank.
>
> Recently, Steve has decided that he would like to sell pet
> supplies at a Sunday flea market in another town, and Scott
> will be in charge of the whole operation.

Eleadari Acheson, 15, writes in GWS no. 76 about her work
at a second-hand bookstore and as a coach at a gymnastics
club:

> During the past two years the store moved to a larger location
> and my hours have increased to three five-hour days per week.
> My income and responsibilities have increased as well. I now
> buy and price books, clean, organize displays, make business
> calls, write business letters, conduct book searches, answer
> questions and restock shelves. In addition, when the owners
> are away I handle mail and banking.
>
> At first I was the only employee, but a few months ago three
> more employees were hired ... As senior employee, I am paid
> more per hour than the rest even though I am the youngest.
> When the owners are unavailable, the other employees call me
> when they have questions ...

About her gymnastics work:

> When I started I wasn't strong enough to spot even a front
> limber with the older kids. Now I'm spotting the older kids'
> back handsprings by myself. I also lead warm-ups and teach
> the less complicated tricks while the head coach teaches the
> harder stuff ... I consider my jobs the most important part of
> my homeschooling education.

Randall Kern writes in *GWS* no. 67:

> I am 12 and have been a homeschooler all my life. I have been
> programming computers for six years. A year ago I started
> going to an IBM computer club, even though I didn't have an
> IBM. When we got one, last June, I became the consultant for
> our group.
>
> The last meeting I went to was held in a newspaper office,
> because the computer they use for their accounting needed to
> be set up. When we got there we found out that the program
> they had bought didn't do what they wanted. So they hired me
> to write an accounts receivable and account maintenance
> program for the newspaper ...

Leonie Edwards, 16, loves her full-time job as a dental
assistant, and plans to become a dentist. She began working
at 14 as a sort of assistant-to-the-assistant. At that time, she
wrote in *GWS* no. 64:

> I work mainly with the dental assistant. I started doing things
> like cleaning rooms, sterilizing instruments, setting up trays,
> preparing the rooms for the next patient, and watching how
> the dental assistant did things. After a while they gave me
> more to do, such as getting the patients in and putting a movie
> on for them, filing, preparing syringes, making sure the rooms
> are stocked and developing x-rays. Then I started assisting the
> dentist with several patients. Now the dentist calls me, instead
> of the dental assistant, to help with fillings and sometimes root
> canals.

'Thanks to homeschooling,' she writes now, 'I can put "two
and a half years of dental assisting experience" on my

college application.' At the same time, she's working on a correspondence course from the University of Kentucky on human biology. This will count towards her pre-dental bachelor's degree.

30 | Your Own Business

The people who get on in this world are the people who get up and look for the circumstances they want, and, if they can't find them, make them.

George Bernard Shaw

Starting a business can mean freedom, creativity, self-expression and fulfillment of your unique talents and interests. It can involve nearly anything: breeding and selling tropical fish, cleaning people's attics, running a bead store, mending old books or jeans, training horses, being a computer or Internet consultant, recording language instruction cassette tapes if you have a native tongue other than English.

In a business, you answer to yourself and your customers (or clients) instead of a boss. Naturally, running your own business means you have to stand on your own two feet, and that nonexistent boss can't give you a salary. If you act wisely and love what you do, you'll probably *eventually* make a profit. If the worst happens, you could lose your investment of money; if your business is something like childcare or petsitting, you could possibly even be sued if a court held you responsible for damages. However, if you take care with whatever you are doing and don't make any empty promises, you should have no trouble.

There are two reasons why starting a business especially suits itself to teenagers. First, you don't yet need to support yourself financially. You needn't worry about making fast money, so you can enjoy a slow start, learning gradually from your mistakes.

Many adults cannot easily afford to go into business, because they can't take the time off their original jobs to get started – and they have to keep those jobs to support themselves. Many businesses make no profit or even lose money their first year or so. This is mainly because most businesses require an initial investment – large or small depending on the type of business, your standards and your ingenuity. Generally, a retail business requires the greatest initial investment – renting premises and buying all the things you plan to sell. (You can cut costs anywhere, of course, if you are creative. I have a tiny retail business with almost no overhead expenses; it consists mainly of bringing a box of sequined veils along every time I teach a dance class or workshop.) At the other end of the spectrum, a service business requires little capital. To be a tutor, freelance photographer, guitar teacher or typist would require only advertising and transportation costs plus the tools of the trade – camera, guitar or wordprocessor.

I do not wish to imply that your business *can't* make a profit in its early stages. Especially if it's your major goal to make money, you can do it. My friend Laura made bread and cookies every day during one of her school years and, by selling them to teachers and students, she paid for a trip to Scotland the following summer.

The second reason starting a business is a great idea for teenagers is that it's one of the few legal, exciting money-making opportunities for people under the age of 18. Many places can't hire you until you're 16, but no one can stop you from running most kinds of businesses. Even if you're 16, finding fun work isn't necessarily easy. There's always McDonald's, but a job like that is for someone who's too tired out – by school, for instance – to do anything better.

For the most part, any business run by an adult could also be a teenage business. Remember, though, not to be limited by anyone's list; just because you've never heard of anyone who has made a business out of helping kids build treehouses and forts doesn't mean it can't be done.

WHEN ARE YOU READY TO START?

It depends on what you want to do. You probably already have some skills that could lead to a business without further training. The people I taught at school, aged 11 to 14, already had the expertise necessary to operate dozens of types of businesses, such as decorating and painting skateboards, teaching or tutoring Japanese or Hebrew, raising and breeding various animals or producing videos.

Perhaps you'd like to do something you're not yet skilled in – but could be with some practice, guidance and/or good tools. A job related to your interests is valuable training for a later business, especially when you're fairly new to the field. Or you can design a more independent training ground. Maybe you're a good tap dancer and would like to start a small professional troupe, but first you want to spend a year or so having more lessons, giving amateur recitals, and studying all the old Gene Kelly and Fred Astaire musicals you can get your hands on. Good. Do it. Yes, it's best to hold out long enough to be sure you're offering your buyers a quality product or service, but don't wait too long just because you have stage fright. Sometimes there comes a point when your interest can't develop any further until you put yourself on the line and start sharing your skill with the world.

To make your business successful on all levels, be sure it is not only something you love and that the public will buy, but also something *good* for people and for this battered planet. I mean not only the *type* of business, but also your approach to it. Run your business under the scrutiny of your own moral code. Mainly, just *think* about what you're doing and take time to do it right. If you open a catering service, consider an alternative to polystyrene foam (Styrofoam, etc) packaging. As a fabric painter, you can find dyes and paints that don't harm water systems after you dump them down the drain. When singing for a crowd, aim not just to impress your listeners, but also to warm them and make them feel good.

Also, remember that a lot of situations that we think of as teenage 'jobs' are really small businesses – when you're babysitting or shoveling snow there's a fine line between 'clients' and 'bosses'. While this sort of work may not be quite as glamorous as designing rock gardens, you can make it more meaningful simply by *thinking* of it as a business and then becoming more creative in your approach to it.

Unschooling can give you an advantage even in these typical teenage 'jobs'. Unschooler Lora Risley mentions in *GWS* no. 76, 'I was allowed to babysit at children's homes and I earned quite a bit of money because I was available when the other babysitters were at school.'

UNSCHOOLERS IN BUSINESS

Amelia Acheson writes in *GWS* no. 42 about her 12-year-old daughter, also Amelia:

> She picked up a clowning book at the library last summer. Her first decision was to duplicate one of the costumes and gags she saw there for a Halloween costume. It turned out so delightful that she was invited to bring it to a day-care center to 'show-off' and entertain the little kids. Over the year, that has grown to a business, and now includes all three of our kids. They have been paid for their clowning – they have their own business cards, they brought home a huge first place trophy from a parade – and, mostly, they have a lot of fun at it. They ride unicycles, juggle, do gymnastics. Tia does magic tricks

(one of her magic books says that magic is a trade like no other – you have to learn it yourself at home). They sometimes work in partnership with a 14-year-old clown from another town who makes balloon animals – as a result, he is learning to unicycle, and they are learning to make balloon animals.

In *GWS* no. 24, a mother tells about her family's unschooling. They'd spent the first year with the Calvert curriculum (a correspondence school) and not especially enjoyed it. So they changed:

> Into the second year, we started the family business. We sell and repair bicycles. We also sell all accessories associated with bicycling. The kids and I manage the store while Dad does his full-time job as a carpenter. (Unless you are very rich, outside income is necessary the first years in business.) He has an active role in the store evenings and weekends. Our 15-year-old son, who has the bike knowledge (from books and other places) manages the repair department, doing all repairs (and training Dad), keeping stock of parts, and working with customers. Our 16-year-old daughter, who is the family organizer, keeps us clean and orderly and manages the store, selling and keeping up with the accessory inventory. Mother's (that's me!) main job is to keep the office going, doing the accounts, etc ... Sounds simple? It's not. But somehow it all works!

At 16, Carmen Rodriguez-Winter and her 17-year-old brother Javier opened their own shop, Back Alley Peddlers, in Toledo, Ohio. They sell secondhand and antique clothing, concert T-shirts, skateboards, hats, their own handmade jewelry, incense, hair dye, poetry written by their friends, lava lamps, and such. Carmen had fantasized about opening her own store when she was only 9 or 10 and still at school, and after a few years out of school (she left when she was 13) she felt ready to do so. With their mother's help, Carmen and Javier decorated and renovated the building and launched their dream, traveling to Los Angeles, New York and Chicago for fashion shows.

'Without homeschool this wouldn't be a reality at all,' Carmen says. 'I'd still be at school, just sitting there, being really super bored, and doing nothing with my life, just being a bum.'

Eighteen-year-old Emily Bergson-Shilcock who lives in Pennsylvania also opened her own shop, The Destination of Independence. She explains:

I was homeschooled all my life. The basic philosophy of my homeschooling education was 'learn in the process of doing real work' (as opposed to 'make work' – like math worksheets instead of purposeful measurement in the wood shop or kitchen) ...

Just after my 17th birthday, I reached my lifelong goal and opened a retail store. I have always been interested in money and business, and my parents have supported my interest – for instance, when I was 10 they gave me a real electronic cash register. Also, starting at age 7 I was involved in numerous volunteer opportunities. Consequently, my life's dream was to discover how I could combine business and helping others into a feasible career.

The Destination of Independence, selling products to make everyday living easier for people with disabilities, was born in April of 1995. My products include wall-mounted jar openers, reachers, long-handled shoe horns, ergonomically designed garden tools, Arthritis Foundation award-winning kitchen utensils and doorknob grips and extensions – all designed and chosen to help people with multiple sclerosis, arthritis, carpal-tunnel syndrome, etc. Owning and managing my store has helped me to broaden my world and educate me in hundreds of ways: researching manufacturers and products, public speaking through demonstrations, writing business letters, handling state and federal taxes, using a financial management system on the computer, increasing my sensitivity to the needs of the elderly and disabled, practicing continuous improvement, and realizing that with hard work and a positive attitude, anything is possible.

I have loved being a homeschooler, not because it is the only way I think one can learn and flourish, but because I think it was the best way for me. Consequently, learning for me is an enjoyable, fulfilling experience. I look forward to entering the class of 2000 and continuing my educational experience at both Beaver College and my store, The Destination of Independence.

Notes

1 John Gatto's acceptance speech as published in *Dumbing Us Down: The Hidden Curriculum of Compulsory Schooling*, New Society Publishers, Philadelphia, 1992, pp 24–5

2 Information from National Home Education Research Institute, PO Box 13939, Salem, OR 97309, USA, tel. 503 364 1490, www.nheri.org.

3 *See* Hein, Hilde S, *The Exploratorium: The Museum as Laboratory*, Smithsonian Institution Press, Washington, DC, 1990

4 *See* Cremin, Lawrence A, *American Education: The National Experience 1783–1876*, Harper and Row, New York, 1980; Good, Harry G, *A History of American Education*, Macmillan, New York, 1962; Kotin, Lawrence, and Aikman, William F, *Legal Foundations of Compulsory School Attendance*, Kennikat Press, Port Washington, NY, 1980

5 Cremin, pp 350–1

6 *Current Biography Yearbook*, H W Wilson and Co, New York, annual

7 *Current Biography Yearbook*, 1988

8 *Current Biography Yearbook*, 1978

9 Sources: *Current Biography Yearbook*; Plent, Malcolm and Nancy, *Famous Homeschoolers*, Graham, Robin Lee, *Dove*, HarperCollins, New York, 1972; various other biographies; *The Norton Anthology of English Literature*, vol 2, Norton, New York, 1972; Prause, Gerhard, *School Days of the Famous*, Springer, New York, 1978

10 Good, p 84

11 *Current Biography Yearbook*, 1979

12 Churchill, Sir Winston, *Great Destiny*, Putnam, London, 1965

13 *Current Biography Yearbook*, 1989

14 Dr John Wesley Taylor's doctoral dissertation 'Self-concept in home-schooling children' and article on same subject in

Home School Researcher, as described in Ray, Dr Brian D, *Marching to the Beat of their Own Drum: A Profile of Home Education Research*, Home School Legal Defense Association, 1992

15   Colfax, David and Micki, *Homeschooling for Excellence*, Warner Books, New York, 1988, p. 46

16   Livezev, Emilie Tavel, 'Self-educated Scientist's Formula for Life-long Discovery', *Christian Science Monitor*, 12.20.1982

17   Lanes, Selma G, *The Art of Maurice Sendak*, Abrams, New York, 1980

18   Sources: *Growing Without Schooling*; personal correspondence and conversation; various colleges' literature; Karl M Bunday's Web site, http://198.83.39/School_is–dead/Learn_in_ freedom.html

19   Sources: *Current Biography Yearbook*; *1979 Book of Lists* Little, New York, 1979; Growing Without Schooling nos 17 and 59

Appendix

FOR EVERYONE: INTERNATIONAL UNSCHOOLING RESOURCES

Books, magazines and mail order

'And What About College?' How homeschooling leads to admissions to the best colleges and universities, by Cafi Cohen, Holt Associates, Cambridge, Massachusetts, 1997.

Cafi's unschooled (definitely not 'schooled at home') son was admitted to the US Air Force Academy – one of the most selective institutions in the US and typically rather rigid in its admissions requirements. Later, her daughter was also admitted to a selective college, and received a substantial merit scholarship. Cafi tells her own family's inspiring story, and also gives extensive, complete information on every aspect of admission to all types of colleges and universities, based on homeschoolers' experiences and also on information from college admissions departments themselves. Though Cafi writes from a US perspective, much of her advice will be useful for unschoolers around the world.

Growing Without Schooling

Published by Holt Associates (*see below*). This outstanding magazine gets better all the time and is chock full of articles and detailed letters from unschooled teenagers, as well as parents and younger children. International in scope and vision, though dominated by US unschoolers. Put this at the top of your shopping list; it will help immeasurably as you begin taking charge of your own education. Currently $25 per year for six thorough issues, from Growing Without Schooling, 2269 Massachusetts Ave, Cambridge, MA 02140, USA, tel. 617 864

3100. Canadian and foreign surface mail orders add $4, add $15 for foreign air mail.

John Holt

I strongly suggest that you read at least one of Holt's books early in your unschooling adventure. His profound, plain, myth-shattering words will serve as a powerful reminder as to why you should be out of school. Good ones to start with are *Freedom and Beyond*, *Instead of Education*, *Teach Your Own* or *A Life Worth Living*.

The Independent Scholar's Handbook: The Indispensable Guide for the Stubborn Intelligence

By Ronald Gross (Ten Speed Press, Berkely, Calafornia, 1993). This excellent, detailed book will help you become an expert in any subject you love, without giving up control to a university or any other institution. Charles Darwin, Albert Einstein and Betty Friedan are among the many independent scholars who have used this approach. Ideal if you want to do intense academic work of the finest order – you *don't* need it if you're not academically inclined.

The Millennium Whole Earth Catalog

Edited by Howard Rheingold (Harper, San Francisco, 1994). The possibilities in life will astound you when you flip through the pages of this huge resource book. Its purpose is to give people 'access to tools' – and so it describes some of the best tools available in hundreds of subjects, from 'invertebrates' to 'mysticism'. These tools are mostly books, but also educational programs (Experiment in International Living), software (Life), magazines (*Puncture*), mail order catalogs (New England Cheesemaking Supply Company) and other great stuff. You don't even have to look up the recommended resources in order to learn a lot from the descriptions and excerpts. (Also, see the earlier out-of-print editions of the *Whole Earth Catalog*, available in many libraries and second-hand book shops.)

Wishcraft: How to Get What You Really Want

By Barbara Sher (Ballantine, New York, 1979). This book helped me write and publish the first edition of *The Teenage Liberation Handbook*, start dancing professionally and muster the courage to give up the wrong career (schoolteaching). It's a powerful resource for anyone, of any age, who wants to design and carry out rewarding projects that further their most passionate interests. Helpful, too, for people who feel unmotivated and not thoroughly excited about anything. (Which is a common temporary problem for new unschoolers, who haven't yet unlearned the school lesson that 'other people run our lives'.)

Camp

Not Back to School Camp

An annual week-long gathering of unschoolers aged 13 to 18, hosted by yours truly. For complete information on the next camp, send $1 or one international reply coupon to NBTSC, PO Box 1014, Eugene, OR 97440, USA.

Mail order services

Genius Tribe

Your author's own mail order book catalog for unschoolers. My husband Skip and I sell only what we consider to be the best books (and videos, tapes, etc) for teaching yourself mathematics, science, foreign languages, writing, etc. Send $1 or one international reply coupon to Genius Tribe, PO Box 1014, Eugene, OR 97440, USA.

John Holt's Bookstore Catalog

Another service of Holt Associates. It offers all John Holt's books and other important books and booklets on unschooling. Free from John Holt's Bookstore, 2269 Massachusetts Ave, Cambridge, MA 02140, USA, tel. 617 864 3100.

Organizations

Clonlara's Home-based Education Program

Clonlara is an umbrella school (*not* a correspondence school) based in Michigan, and it serves unschoolers in all 50 states of the US and around the world. If you feel isolated and want some good long-distance support, or if you would like someone else to help you keep records and handle all the negotiations with your school board or other authorities, I highly recommend this organization. After you complete their resonable, extremely flexible requirements they will even award you a bona fide high school diploma. The Home Based Education Program, Clonlara School, 1289 Jewel, Ann Arbor, MI 48104, USA, www.grfn.org/education/clonlara, tel. 313 769 4515, CLONLARA@delphi.com.

Holt Associates

These amazing, knowledgeable people were friends and colleagues of John Holt, the pioneer of unschooling in the US. They continue his work, publish the excellent magazine *Growing Without Schooling* (*see above*) and have amassed decades of experience with hundreds of unschoolers. If you have questions, they offer excellent, reasonably priced consultations over the phone or in person. They have a good section on Compuserve; you can browse their library (Go EdProB), send e-mail (76202.3703@compuserve.com) or chat – check their section for live chat schedule Holt Associates, 2269 Massachusetts Ave, Cambridge, MA 02140, USA, tel. 617 864 3100.

Directory Issue of Growing Without Schooling

The annual directory issue of *GWS* is published each January but is available year-round. It provides addresses of hundreds of homeschooling organizations in all 50 states and around the world. It also lists related organizations, including umbrella schools, correspondence schools and other private schools that help homeschoolers. Better yet, this directory includes thousands of homeschooling families, organized by state and country – most are in the US but there are hundreds of others also, representing 32 countries in all. If you can't find an organization listed for your country, you can usually get information from one of the families in this extensive directory. $6.00 (plus postage if you're outside the US – surface $1, airmail $3) from Holt Associates, 2269 Massachusetts Ave., Cambridge, MA 02140.

Web sites

Jon Shemitz's 'Jon's Homeschool Resource' page, www. midnightbeach.com/hs/
Karl M. Bunday's 'School is Dead/Learn in Freedom' page http://198.83.19.39/School_is_dead/Learn_in_freedom.html
The Home Education Press page (includes information on laws in all 50 states of the US), www.home-ed-press.com/wlcm_hsinf. hmtl
The Homeschooling Zone (includes a worldwide directory of homeschoolers), www.caro.net/~joespa/
The Canadian Alliance of Homeschoolers (good worldwide links), www.netroute.net/~altpress/ds/cahs.html
See also Holt Associates.

SPECIFIC COUNTRIES

(If your country isn't listed, contact Clonlara – *see above*.)

American military families

Consult DoD Manual 1342.6-M and UR 10–12.
Contact Valerie Bonham Moon at HQs USAREUR, CMR 420, Box 606, APO AE 09063, starrmoon@hotmail.com.

Australia

Homeschoolers Australia Pty Ltd PO Box 420, Kellyville, NSW 2153, tel. 02 6293727.
Eleanor Sparks's Australian Home Schooling Resource Page, www.3dproductions.com.au/homeschool/
The Australian Home Education page, http://cs.anu.edu.au/people/Drew.Corrigan/home_ed/overview.html

Canada

The Canadian Homeschool Resource page (outstanding and comprehensive), www.flora.org/homeschool-ca/
The Canadian Alliance of Home Schoolers, 272 Hwy #5, RR 1, St George, ON N0E 1N0, tel. 519 448 4001, www.netroute.net/~altpress/ds/cahs.html.
Virtual High and the WonderTree Education Society, PO Box 3803, Vancouver, BC, V5Z 4L9, tel. 604 739 5941, http://bc-education.botany.ubc.ca/vh/vh.html. (These are outstanding 'independent schools' for British Columbian unschoolers.)
The Calgary Montessori Home Education Program, Community Connections, 101 Point Drive, NW, Calgary, AB T3B 5C8. (An excellent program for Albertans.)

France

Les Enfants d'Abord, c/o Shosha, 4 rue de League, F–34800 Brignac, tel. 4 67 96 90 44 (alternative address: c/o Grde Rue, Valence 26000).

Germany

Valerie Bonham Moon (from an American military family), HQs USAREUR, CMR 420, Box 620, APO AE 09063, starrmoon@ hotmail.com.

New Zealand

Homeschooling Federation of New Zealand PO Box 41 226, St Lukes, Auckland.
New Zealand Home Schoolers' Association (NZHSA), PO Box 41-226 St Lukes, Auckland, tel./fax 09 849 4780.

Ireland

Sa Baile, c/o Theresa Murphy, Clahane, Ballard, Tralee, Co Kerry.
Or c/o Marguerite Egan, Cillmhicadomhnaigh, Ventry, Co Kerry.

Japan

Otherwise Japan, PO Box Kugayama, Suginama-ku, Tokyo, JAB02521@niftyserve.or.jp.

Netherlands

Netherlands Homeschoolers, Raadhuislaan 31, 2131 Hoofddoorp.
The Alternative Learning Exchange, http://mcs.nl/ale/ale-3.html#contents

South Africa

National Coalilition of Home Schoolers, PO Box 14, Dundee, 3000 tel. 0341 23712, durham@liadun.dundee.lia.net.

Spain

Crecer Sin Escuela, c/o Norberg-Szil, Apdo 45, E–03580 l'Alfás del Pi, Alicante.

Switzerland

Marie Heitzmann, Au Village 12, 1277 Borex.
Les Enfants D'Abord, Relations Internationales, Claudia Gringmann, impasse Jean Pierre, 66130 Trevillach, France.

United Kingdom

Education Otherwise, PO Box 7420, London N9 9SG, tel. 01926 886828, www.educate.co.uk/edother.htm
Education Now, 113 Arundel Drive, Bramcote Hills, Nottingham NG9 3FQ, tel. 0115 925 7261
Home Education Advisory Service, PO Box 98, Welwyn Garden City, Herts. AL8 6AN, http://ourworld.compuserve.com/ homepages/home_ed_advisory_srv
Advice for Home Educators in England and Wales, www.educate.co.uk/leaninfo.htm.

United States

Holt Associates, 2269 Massachusetts Ave, Cambridge, MA 02140, tel. 617 864 3100, 76202.3703@compuserve.com.
Jon Shemitz's 'Jon's Homeschool Resource Page', www.midnightbeach.com/hs/
Karl M Bunday's 'School is Dead/Learn in Freedom' page, http://198.83.19.39/School_is_dead/Learn_in_freedom.html
The Home Education Press page (includes information on laws in all 50 states), www.home-ed-press.com/wlcm_hsinf.hmtl

Bibliography

Abrams, MH, *A Glossary of Literary Terms,* Harcourt Brace College Publications, Orlando, Florida, 1993

Adams, Ansel, *Examples: The Making of Forty Photographs,* Bulfinch, New York, 1989

Alexander, Christopher, *A Pattern Language,* Oxford University Press, NY, 1977

Arem, Cynthia, *Conquering Math Anxiety,* Brooks-Cole, Pacific Grove, California, 1992

Bauermeister, Erica, *Five Hundred Great Books by Women,* Penguin, NY, 1994

Berry, Wendell, *Standing By Words,* North Point, Berkeley, California, 1983

Campbell, Joseph, with Moyers, Bill, *The Power of Myth,,* Doubleday, NY, 1988

Colfax, David and Micki, *Homeschooling for Excellence,* Warner Books, New York, 1988

Collins, Nancy, *Professional Women and Their Mentors, ,* Prentice Hall, Englewood Cliffs, NJ, 1983

Concise Science Dictionary, Oxford University Press, Oxford, 3rd edition, 1996

Fadiman, Clifton A, *The Lifetime Reading Plan,* HarperCollins, NY, 1988

Fire, John (Lame Deer), *Lame Deer, Seeker of Visions,* Simon and Schuster, NY, 1973

Fry, Ronald W., *Internships: Newspaper, Magazine, and Book Publishing,*

Goldberg, Natalie, *Wild Mind,* Bantam, NY, 1990

– *Writing Down the Bones,* Shambhala, Boston, 1986

Graham, Robin Lee, *Dove,* Harper and Row, NY, 1972

Gross, Ronald, *The Independent Scholar's Handbook: The Indispensable Guide for the Stubborn Intelligence,* Ten Speed Press, Berkeley, California, 1993

Hailey, Kendall, *The Day I Became An Autodidact*, Dell, NY, 1988

Holt, John, *Freedom and Beyond*, Heinemann, Portsmouth, New Hampshire, 1972

– *Instead of Education*, Holt Associates, Boston, 1976

– *A Life Worth Living*, Ohio State University Press, Columbus, Ohio, 1990

– *Teach Your Own*, Dell, NY, 1981

Internships: on-the-job training opportunities for college students and adults

Kenda, and Williams, *Math Wizardry for Kids*, Margaret Kenda and Phyllis Williams, Barron's, Hauppage, New York, 1995

Joudry, Patricia, *And the Children Played*, Tundra, Plattsburg, New York, 1975

Lame Deer *see* Fire, John

The Norton Anthology of American Literature, WW Norton, NY, 6th edition, 1997

The Norton Anthology of English Literature, WW Norton, NY, 6th edition, 1997

The Norton Introduction to Literature, WW Norton, NY, 1982

Rheingold, Howard (ed), *The Millennium Whole Earth Catalog*, HarperSanFrancisco, San Francisco, 1994 and *The Next Whole Earth Catalog*, Random, NY, 1980

Rico, Gabrielle, *Writing the Natural Way*, Tarcher, New York, 1983

Robertson, Laurel, *Laurel's Kitchen*, Bantam, NY, 1976

Rucker, Rudy, *Mind Tools: The Five Levels of Mathematical Reality*, Houghton Mifflin, NY, 1988

Sher, Barbara, *Wishcraft: How to Get What You Really Want*, Ballantine, New York, 1979

Stevenson, Robert Louis, *Crabbed Age and Youth in Essays and Poems*, Tuttle, NY, 1993

Strunk, and White, *The Elements of Style*, Macmillan, NY, 1979

Thoreau, Henry David, *Walden*, 1854, Penguin, NY, 1983

Tobias, Sheila, *Overcoming Math Anxiety*, HarperCollins, NY, 1995

Index